MW01290571

The Providence Factor

When God Shapes a World Changer

Jim Beaird

Copyright © 2015 James M. Beaird

All rights reserved.

ISBN: **1511673885**
ISBN-13: **978-1511673884**

TriFactor
PUBLISHING

Dedication and Acknowledgements

Dedicated to my wonderful wife, Kris, whose
unbroken support and critique provided motivation
to produce this second book in a series on effective
leadership in the Body of Christ. It's long been her
desire for me to write this series on Providence in
book form.

My deepest appreciation to Ray Smith, my pastor
and former President of Open Bible Churches.
During an especially difficult time earlier in ministry,
Ray placed a providential call to me that made the
difference in me remaining in the ministry.

To Dr. Chuck Stevens, my close friend and colleague
who spoke into my life long ago during my
Freshman year in college. His words were both
providential and prophetic.

To my son Nate for his skillful application of cover
design and layout. I appreciate his creative talents.

Finally, I'd like to thank Nancy Vencill for her
skillful assistance in the final edit of this book.

Jim Beaird

CONTENTS

Introduction

Most people entertain hypothetical imaginations of their life in terms of what *could have been* against what actually exists in the present. Perhaps, in a reflective moment, they wondered what would have happened had they made different choices in their education, job selection, marriage, circle of friends, family planning, and a myriad of other significant events of the past. Some live in a perpetual state of disillusionment with life—wondering if things will ever improve or if they have any power to change what *is* to what they think they want.

A poorly-defined set of self-expectations often drives the quest for fulfillment and significance as they try to make sense out of their present reality. Through the course of their life to the present, one day simply seemed to merge into the next until much of their life was in the rear-view mirror and getting further and further away. They don't really understand what is ahead because they did not fully understand the trajectory they traveled to bring them to the "right now" of life. So, for far too many, life just continues without any understanding of how one's life events correspond to each other to produce the picture that rightly describes and illustrates God's design for how they are to impact their world.

Failure to understand their lot in life fuels the poor perception of the possibilities that exist in the life of an individual who accepts the inter-relationship of every event of their life. Every event. Whether they realize it or not, each event is like a piece of a puzzle and without that event, the puzzle of their life would be incomplete. A puzzle with missing pieces produces a profound disappointment when all other pieces are in place. Only a partial picture emerges from the hours of assembly. Each piece has its role in the final revelation of beauty and symmetry intended by the artist.

The surety of God's providence does not guarantee total acceptance or understanding in the course of human events. A beautiful tapestry provides partial understanding of God's process of weaving inter-related events into a finished product capable of revealing His purposes in the design of His creation and in His children. He often withholds the unveiling of the final tapestry until everything He needed to accomplish in our lives is complete. The events of our lives are a part of His creation and He uses everything as strands to weave beauty and purpose into a product that will glorify and honor Him. During the process, He only lets us see the backside of the tapestry of our life. No apparent design characterizes the intent of His work as we see only strands running this way and that—with no discernable form and no recognizable image in mind. What we see is the messy side of His process in our lives. The strands on the backside of the tapestry emerge from underneath other strands then return to the "hidden mess" from which we vainly try to guess what he's trying to produce. We see only knots and junctions in our inability to see as He sees us. The backside of a tapestry looks like a series of failures and messes. Ugliness leers back at us as we try to discover a pattern from which we can imagine the finished product.

1 Corinthians 13: 12b states, "Now I know in part, but then shall I know just as I also am known." If we believe the Word of God to be true and reliable, we must accept the fact that He does not want us to know how things are supposed to work ahead of time. If we did, our natural propensity would compel us to control the eventual outcome and ruin the finished product being transmitted from the mind of the Father into the reality of our life as

living vessels capable of honoring Him.

When I was a child I noticed a cocoon hanging on the lilac bush beside the patio in the back yard. Curiosity drew my full attention as I eventually broke the branch twig off and took it to the picnic table. As I sat watching, I noticed that it was moving. The longer I watched, the more intense the cocoon's movement became. I began to grow anxious about whatever was trapped inside. I suspected that it was a butterfly since many had invaded the area in recent days. So, I reasoned that I could set it free and eliminate the struggle. I could help the little guy and he'd be grateful for my help. I produced a pocketknife from my pocket (we were allowed to carry them back then) and proceeded to carefully open the cocoon. After my liberating surgery the cocoon fell away and a wet, mostly limp butterfly plopped out. I remember feeling elated at the great task I had just completed and prompted the butterfly to spread out its wings and fly away. But, rather than cheering it in its maiden flight, I watched in adolescent horror as it simply quit moving and died.

I told my dad about the butterfly and my attempts to free it from its prison. He told me that butterflies need the time of struggle inside the cocoon to strengthen their wings and prepare them for their short lifespan. He said that when it can break out of its cocoon, it's ready to begin its life— but not before. I had actually ended its life by trying to eliminate an essential process in gaining its freedom and being a thing of beauty. I thought I was helping but instead, my efforts produced only death and a short circuit of what God had intended for a small part of His creation. God had a proven process. I intervened and ruined it.

That memory serves as a reminder of necessary struggles and their intended outcomes. God has a purpose for everything in our lives. Nothing happens without first receiving His permission. His will for us is to grow through the struggle and gain confidence in His unfailing ability to redeem any situation. We learn that struggles are actually a part of His plan to grow us into overcomers who stand firm in the face of trial and adversity and eventually encourage others in the struggles they encounter. There is no waste in God's plan.

Long before Joshua led the people into the promised land, an account in Genesis begins an elaborate unwinding of Hebrew history to the point that one must wonder why God would do what He did—allow their history to start in a place, transplant them, and then to re-deposit them in the land of their origins. God didn't need to prepare a new place—just a new time and a willing people. The time that God used to prepare them was rife with struggles, hardship, and pain. As we glance back into that historical era, we must understand that those people did not have the convenience of gadgets and probability studies to determine their present social and economic condition. They had only their belief that God alone controlled their destiny and ultimately, He had the last word. They lived only to survive and live another day.

This book takes a linear view of history and illustrates how one historical event actually becomes a strand connected to other events on the backside of life's tapestry. The intended result? An intricately woven arras revealing the work of a master designer who wove significant events in and out of our lives and produced a beautiful illustration of His purpose for His people. Specifically, the account of Joseph, his brothers, his family, and their intertwined destiny provides the setting for helping us understand the miracle of God's providence as He uses entire lifetimes to illustrate the beauty and provision of His intended plan for all mankind.

Chapter 1

The Dreamer

Genesis 37 begins the longest cycle of historical accounts recorded in Genesis. Scholars are fairly certain that chapters 37-47 are the work of one author. Because that is so, the Joseph story provides a complete narrative. Other narratives in Genesis provide a historical porthole through which we can gain insight and understanding of various segments of Hebrew history. However, the story of Joseph provides a larger porthole revealing pivotal junctures in the survival of an entire race of people.

A Limited View

The tapestry's backside provides a curious hodge-podge of knots and apparent mistakes. The front side of the tapestry would later reveal the skilled hand of a sovereign designer—a providential planner who knows which event must be connected to another to produce his intended result.

Verse 1 begins,

"Now Jacob dwelt in the land where his father was a stranger, in the land of Canaan."

Whereas Isaac and Abraham had maintained temporary residence in the Promised Land, Jacob and his heirs live there permanently. Prior to their move to Egypt (which we will discuss later on), they had occupied an area of Canaan for 193 years, settled in Egypt for another nearly 100 years and were emancipated from their slave-like conditions under the leadership of Moses around 1445 B.C.

Why this little historical side-trip? I'd like to go back to the time that Jacob's family originally lived in the land of promise. A series of events that shaped Israel's history will also give us additional insight into what God has in store for each of us today. Sometimes a rear-view can explain a lot. We just need a glance backward to understand God's providence. While the part of life we see often looks confusing, it is a part of a larger picture—a masterpiece wherein each apparent insignificancy of our life becomes a vital component of God's provision, protection, and providence. So it is with the narrative of Joseph. As we will discover later, his life's promise and potential gave way to a perplexing twist of fate, which he would not understand until many years later.

In this 37th chapter of Genesis, the author focuses on Joseph, the child of Rachel, Jacob's best-loved wife. Joseph's character profile emerges as less than desirable. The second verse records that Joseph brought a bad report about his other brothers. All the sons of Jacob are shepherds—except the youngest one. The "bad report" he brought to his father reveals that he must have been a spoiled tattletale. Many have grown up with a tattletale sibling intent upon getting them into trouble. When a child senses his parents value him above his siblings, an unfair advantage emerges in which insulation against punishment provides an alternate path for behavioral development. Perhaps, the favored sibling feels immune to the same guidelines and eventual punishment that keeps brothers and sisters from straying from the established set of family or societal expectations. Why Joseph tattled on his brothers is not fully clarified here, but it offers us a glimpse into the character of a spoiled child. Maybe his father had asked him to spy on his brothers and discretely report anything out of the ordinary. He probably relished his father's favor and felt secure in his covert role among his brothers.

Directly after we hear that Joseph is some sort of "spy" among his brothers, we learn that he was given a robe—as the translators to English from the Latin Vulgate termed, "a coat of many colors." While we try to imagine what that garment must have looked like, we generally picture it as a very colorful full length tunic held together in the front by a matching cloth belt. Joseph wore it with pride knowing its design garnered the attention of anyone looking in his general direction. However, the original language made no reference to color. Rather, it had to do with a distinctive and elaborate garment, which became the very symbol of Jacob's obsessive love toward Joseph—a symbol that only caused the hatred from his brothers to increase in intensity.

When the brothers saw it, they could not even speak peaceably with him. In language we can understand today—they hated the little tattletale twit. Bad situation! They knew he had somehow gained his father's favor—even though they did all the work tending the flocks in the heat and cold of the region's volatile climate. Joseph got to stay home, enjoying the comfortable surroundings and basking in his father's generosity.

Things go from bad to worse. Joseph begins to dream and can hardly wait to reveal the content of these dreams to his family. How do you think that played out? His brothers only hated him all the more. It's not bad enough to have to listen to the little twerp, now he asserts his alleged dominion over them through his dreams—you know, the dreams he probably had while they were out in the countryside attending the family's flocks.

The Final Straw

The first dream showed sheaves of grain standing in a field. Each sheaf represented one of his brothers. His sheaf stood up straight and all the others bowed down to his. Telling his brothers this was like throwing gasoline on a burning fire. BOOM! They react explosively and ask, "You really think you will rule over us?"

Joseph can't leave it alone. He has another dream in which the sun, moon and 11 stars bowed down to him. Of course, he *had* to tell them about this one, as well. Not only did his brothers begin to manifest a piqued resentment toward him, but his father joined in censuring him for his impetuous and reckless posturing in the family order. As things start to get out of hand, Jacob engaged in a bit of damage control. His older sons need to know their father realized the situation and was willing to confront his favorite offspring. Verse 10 records his father's rebuke. The verb for "rebuke" in this verse is used to describe God's shouts to the sea, or at the nations. It is a powerful way of communicating an imperative. We must assume his father used the strongest possible language to assuage his family's frustration at his young son's insistence on keeping his brothers in a constant state of resentment.

At this point in the narrative, Joseph is portrayed for us as an arrogant young man who doesn't know when to stop. We have already read this passage in scripture about the trials and tribulations that ensued from Joseph's general demeanor and self-aggrandizement. We have always seen the narrative as a whole and therein we know what is coming and how things eventually turned out for Joseph and his family.

What we *don't* factor in are the threads of providence being woven into the tapestry of Joseph's life and the eventual beauty God designed in its completion. We must understand that God weaves seemingly insignificant strands of unusual color and texture into our lives every day. He alone sees our tapestry's front side and He alone understands the degree to which we will need to experience both the pleasant and the unpleasant. He weaves strands of agony and ecstasy together to help us understand the balance that real life demands. He weaves strands of hope with strands of disillusionment to keep us from being too pessimistic or too idealistic. With every positive emotion He weaves an awareness of an antithetical possibility that might prevent us from realizing life's potential.

Joseph's assertion of dominance over his brothers and family fueled the simmering hatred of his brothers in which they began to talk about ways to shut him up. Perhaps they had long discussions in which they elaborated ways to rid themselves of this constant reminder of their father's favoritism and blind love.

Verse 12 tells us that his brothers went to tend their father's flocks in Shechem. The distance from their father's home in Hebron to Shechem was a long distance—60 miles—or about a week's journey one way. Israel sent Joseph on an information-gathering trip. He wanted to know if all was well with his sons.

An Ill-Fated Journey

Consider the task requested of Joseph by his father. Take a weeklong journey, check on his brothers, and report back to dear old dad. He went to Shechem only to find out they had departed for Dothan—eight more miles away or about another day and a half of travel.

In verse 18 of chapter 37, his brothers saw him coming from a distance. It did not take them long to put an already-discussed plan into play. Their plan included killing him and then telling their father a wild beast had killed him. Hopefully, his condescending dreams and "favorite-son" status would die with him. They began to envision life without the continual comparison to "the dreamer."

Their actions were about to manifest the fruit of resentment that had grown deep in their hearts. Resentment drives an insatiable quest for settling the score and evening the playing field. It distorts perspective and instills a myopic view of the end game. It blurs focus on healthy relationships and nurtures a strong desire for vengeance. It drives its roots deep into the heart of a man intent on righting perceived wrongs and punishing the infraction with a biased sense of justice. It robs an individual of peace and replaces it with depression that sucks from them their very life. Irrationality becomes the norm as rationality gets dismissed as too weak to deal with the situation. Resentment never sits dormant in a heart. Rather, it compounds its hold on the individual by binding them with cords of despair and hopelessness.

An interesting subplot emerges from the interplay between the brothers. As the brothers seize Joseph, something unexpected happens. In the midst of all this plotting, the eldest son, Reuben, speaks up. He convinces them not to kill Joseph, but rather throw him into a pit—*then* decide what they'll do with him. Evidently, Reuben arrived after Joseph had already been bound by his older brothers.

Reuben displays an unusual kindness toward his little brother. He was recognized as leader and could have been in line for his father's blessing. However, an interesting event occurred back in chapter 35 that suggests a possible reason for Reuben's change of heart.

> *"While Israel lived in that land, Reuben went in and slept with Bilhah, his father's concubine; and Israel heard about it."* 35:22

To sleep with the concubines and wives of the leader of the community was far more than a sexual act; it was political and announced the desire of the perpetrator to take control of the community. Reuben's act with Bilhah made him repulsive to his father. So—out of his desire to save Joseph, or because of his responsibility as first-born, he sees Joseph as his meal ticket back into the favor of his father. Was Reuben being kind or was he seizing the opportunity to regain his place of blessing with his father? The intent of his heart cannot be discerned from the text provided, but we can surmise that he had a weak stomach for actually killing his brother. He might once have had sex with his father's concubine, but this potential act of murder fell into a much more severe category.

The brothers accept Reuben's advice. They strip the fancy robe from Joseph and throw him in a dry well. While they were thinking about what to do next, Judah suggested selling him to the Ishmaelite traders and *make* some money on the deal. Evidently, Reuben had something to do so he left them to ponder the plan. At lunchtime, they looked up and saw some Midianite and Ishmaelite traders on the road in the distance. They promptly pulled Joseph from the pit and closed the deal for twenty shekels of silver. "Better get this deal closed before Reuben gets back!"

Upon Reuben's return, Joseph was gone. In anguish, he tears his clothes and shouts, "Where shall I go?" His meal ticket back into his father's favor was gone. Perhaps Reuben left his brothers so he could think about a new plan. After all, if he could only get Joseph back to his father, he could regain his place in the family line of succession.

Kindness does not always come from a kind heart. In Reuben's case, his kindness was prompted by an ulterior motive. God alone knows a man's heart. Since there was a bigger plan in play within the realm of God's providence, Reuben's plan did not take precedence over God's. Man can hide behind the façade of good intent, but God knows what lies beneath the shiny veneer of an apparent act of kindness. Reuben's plan was, indeed, not an act of kindness but of self-preservation.

The brothers still had the fancy robe. They dipped it in animal blood and tore it appropriately as to look like an attack by a beast. They traveled back to their own land and held it before their father for identification. Recognizing the robe, Israel refused to be comforted and said, *"No, I will go down to Sheol to my son, mourning." (37:35)*

Joseph is far away and far from being dead. He has been sold into slavery—not to work in the quarries nor on the great Egyptian building projects, but as a household slave to a rich and powerful man, Potiphar, a captain of Pharaoh's personal staff of bodyguards.

While his brothers thought they'd seen the last of Joseph, their relationship with him was by no means over. His story had just begun! The story of God's redemption of His people was just beginning. The tapestry of Joseph's life was on God's loom and He had great plans for the young dreamer. For the next decade and a half, Joseph was only permitted to see the backside of the tapestry of his life. He would only see the knots and apparent failures and wonder why this whole bizarre scenario had to be played out in his life.

Gone forever was the comfort of his father's home and the favor he once enjoyed there. Gone forever was the little brother who did not have the sense to know when to stop talking. Gone forever was the band of brothers who played a major role in the drama he now lived. Gone forever were the assurances his culture provided him about his eventual role in their midst. Gone forever were any plans he might once have had. The loom tightens then expands. Varied strands join other strands already woven into the mystery of what the other side would one day reveal. His tapestry was the destiny of an entire race of people.

Doing Life in Real-Time:

We might ask several questions of ourselves in response to this passage.

1. Do we delight in the misfortune of those we despise?

   Even in church circles, bad news is often more enticing than good news. It depends on where our heart is. What is the ulterior motive of our kindness? Do we use people to get ahead—under the guise of caring for them?

2. Do we measure God's over-all plan by the yardstick of our own experience and understanding?

   What prevents God from accomplishing His will in our lives—at least, in the time frame He desires? We must understand something. Time is on God's side. If we will not respond to Him, He will simply wait for another time, in perhaps another setting, and begin again. If we say, "He has to do it in a way with which I'm familiar," we limit the scope of His power and creative nature. Do you place restrictions on the manner in which God works in your life?

3. Are we guilty of conspiracy against those over us in authority at work?

We can speak evil with our insinuations about them. Maybe they *are* a jerk but are we guilty of undercutting or demeaning their authority? Have we vocalized the feelings that we could do a better job if the responsibility fell in our lap?

4. Are we guilty of character assassination or stealing from a person's value in the minds of our fellow workers?

An individual can do great harm to how another person is perceived by his/her fellow workers. God holds us accountable for each word we speak that demeans another member of His creation. Perhaps the work He seeks to do in their life is hindered by what you have said about them.

5. What about our relationship with those of our own family?

You cannot change them. You can only change what is in your own heart. For *that* you'll have to give account to God. Understand that members of the same family have different gifts and abilities. Not everyone will utilize opportunities in the same measure. Some will waste their gifts through non-use or non-development. Others will strive to develop what they *do* possess and achieve as much or more as the gifted family member. Additionally, they will gain a greater understanding of what it means to understand God's divine and providential plan for their lives.

I have a younger brother who is musically talented and athletic. As I observed his transition through the various phases of his life, I found myself envying him and even being self-righteous in our relationship. I did not feel he lived up to his potential. While I excelled in sports in high school, he was still the better athlete and could easily top me in almost any sport we chose. He was the "natural" and I was the one who had to work hard to be where he was already. While at my home one evening, we had a severe disagreement and ended up in the garage. Neither of us was sure what was going to happen, but our impasse came to a head and we felt the need to resolve it. As we started talking, the strangest thing happened. I was sure that he felt superior to me in sports and that he would relate that to me during the course of the conversation. Instead, he told me that he always felt he was in my shadow and could never measure up to what I had accomplished. I didn't know that. He was so natural and I had to work so hard—just to be at the same place. To this day, we both cite that conversation as a time of clearing the air between us, gaining a truthful perspective of each other, and becoming life-long best friends.

We don't know the full story about our *own* life, let alone the lives of those around us. We have no way of knowing what the future will bring. We have to trust in God—and God alone! Our lives are on God's big loom. He is choosing the colors and textures that will produce the composite of His final product in our lives.

Perhaps in your life there is that person you feel robbed you of the favor you felt you really deserved. Maybe a situation has produced in you resentment and caused a bitter root to grow that now strangles your joy. You've even contemplated taking your own life as a way to get even.

Perhaps, in your perspective, a church hurt you somewhere along the line. That kept you from wanting to get close to the people in it again. You don't know the whole story. God is crafting you in a special way. When He is finished, there will be none other like you.

Here's Your Handle:

Trust God and let life play out. Things are not always as they appear. There is always another side to the belief you've held about someone.

Chapter 2

"Falsely Accused but Rightly Imprisoned"

The beginning of chapter 39 resumes where the end of chapter 37 left the narrative about Joseph and his amazing adventure. The Egyptians purchased Joseph from the Ishmaelites. The Egyptian who bought Joseph was a captain of Pharaoh's personal bodyguard. While Joseph could have ended up in the brickyard making bricks with all the other slaves, God chose to place him in an unusually elevated position in the house of a venerated Egyptian man.

Joseph must have wondered why the predictability of his comfortable life had taken such a drastic turn. First the plots against him by his own brothers and then the transport to Egypt where he was immediately placed on the auction block as human commodity. Then, having been sold to some important guy who dressed like a soldier, he must have thought, "Oh Great! They're going to draft me into their army." But the man was not an army officer. In fact, he worked for Pharaoh as one of his protectors. His shackles are removed as he accompanied the man to his residence. Once there, the man he will come to know as Potiphar gave him new clothes, great food, and charge over his household. Joseph must have thought, "What am I missing? *This* is the life of a slave?"

We'll see a certain phrase over and over again—*"The Lord was with Joseph."* We will learn a great deal about God's sovereignty and providence in Joseph's life and how God intricately wove strands of differing textures and colors into the life of His servant. The eventual design of Joseph's life will prove to have a providential rather than an aesthetic purpose. God does some things just for the beauty of it—just because He can. Other things are woven into a beautiful and elaborately planned tapestry in which things of the past blend with things of the present and, ultimately—things of the future.

Remember, our vantage point in the process of gaining a personal tapestry is behind the actual tapestry itself. All we can see are knots and strands running this way and that with no discernable purpose or design. It is at the rear of the tapestry that God searches the heart of His child and discerns what character formation will emerge from the process and be revealed in the final product.

Beginning to Understand Providence

Do you know what **"providence"** is? It literally means the "loving guidance of God." It refers to His ability to know the future and build into our lives what's best for us and what serves His purpose. We do not respond to the Father like mind-numbed actors or mindless robots. We respond to His love. Once we know that He lovingly guides and facilitates areas of growth in our lives (things we usually call "trials and tribulations"), we accept the process of the Master Weaver and give Him permission to facilitate transformative change in us.

Providence takes into account our **desires** and **dreams**, but doesn't always indulge us in those areas because either the process or the product could leave us short of God's plan. Submission to a plan we did not conceive usually produces a tentative acknowledgement at best. But for the child of God who desires only God's best, certainty of purpose guides the mindset that would otherwise be distracted or disgruntled with the timeframe or intended design. God intends for the heart of His child to be conformed to His. Anything else abrogates the whole process. While His children stand behind the tapestry He's weaving for their life, they must be confident of his sovereignty and reliant on His providence.

Sovereignty and providence do not have to be some theological concept understood only by those who sink years into the study of the Word of God. Actually, providence is one of the most easily understood processes in the entire Bible. It is only difficult to understand because we have made it so. God wants us to embrace His providence so we can be more interested in the *product* than the *process*. We tend to derail things that do not go according to our pre-conceived plans. However, once we gain confidence that God knows what He is doing, we gain perseverance in the *process* and infinitely more interest in the final *product*.

I said it was easy. But, I do not imply that it is for non-structured, 'everything goes' theology that makes it simple for an individual to comply with God's ultimate design. There is still a time of personal application in which the individual must rightly discern God's hand upon their life and willingly submit to His course of action. It will always emerge as a decision to engage God's process in God's timeframe, in God's manner. Back to easy. I must add that our understanding can gain ease, but *simplicity* simply will not exist in the process. In fact, the whole trajectory of an individual's personal spiritual development demands *intricate complexity* known only to God.

When teaching on the subject of God's sovereignty and providence, I ask people to remember three four-word sentences. These sentences wrap the concept of God's providence neatly into a central, personal nugget of understanding designed to keep on track the tapestry's weaving and design.

The sentences are:

God has a plan. He knows what's ahead.
He's shaping a world-changer.

What does believing God require? Most people equate believing God with adherence to certain theological premises laid out by someone else at another time in history. We read of God's exploits in the Old Testament and form a belief that allows miracles to happen *then*, but not necessarily *now*. We believe that God did those things because we believe that His Word is inspired and that it is for us today—even if He does not do miracles in the *same manner* as He did during earlier historical eras. But, believing God is much more than simply agreeing with an historical account of His dealings with mankind. It is in believing the active plan He is working out right now, right here in our lives.

If a person cannot trust God for an active, living involvement in their life, they have an incomplete perception of who God is and how He wants to craft us and use us. The obedient child's mentality needs to center on trusting God for an acceptance of His plan for their life. This is where most people cross wires with God. They try to recapture what they once surrendered to God and argue in favor of their own understanding of how things should proceed. The event in time—in which they once professed their undying trust in God, gets clouded with uncertainty. While once they had actually surrendered their life to God, things now do not seem to be moving at an acceptable pace.

This is precisely where trust must *yield* to obedience. Obedience is that certain quality of relationship with the Father in which blind trust produces the resolve that takes the child of God through the "valley of the shadow of death" and into the light of His presence. Samuel told King Saul, " . . . to obey is better than sacrifice," (1 Sam. 15:22). King Saul took things out of God's hands because he really did not trust God's method for leading His people. So he, in his self-righteousness, performed a sacrifice that was only to be offered by one of God's priests. While he began his rule in humility, he eventually gained enough self-confidence to insert his own decision-making into the mix. Saul trusted God, but he was not obedient. His disobedience caused his own rejection by God as King of Israel.

While God faithfully provides guidelines to follow in fulfilling our part in the process, He does not provide us with a view of the process itself. That is the *trust* part. If He gave us the whole plan up front, we would find a way to bypass the difficulties designed to build character into us and gravitate rather to an easier, more predictable route to the finish line. His process *demands* both trust and obedience. He has one prescribed way in which He lovingly guides through difficult episodes designed by the enemy to defeat us and make us lapse into distrust of the Master Designer. Alternate paths ending in success simply do not exist. If we take things out of His hands, we immediately short-circuit His plan and mar His beautiful design of what He plans to accomplish through our obedience.

What about predestination?

When we talk about God's providence and sovereignty, we naturally feel our minds being drawn like nails to a magnet to the subject of *predestination.* Some theologies believe that mankind is predestined to either accept or reject Christ. A minister once told me there will be many pastors who lead others to Christ, look after the needs of a church congregation, devoutly serve God, yet, will not enter into a heavenly reward because they will find out they are not one of the "elect." While I held the minister in high regard, I could not help but wonder if I would be one of those who got to the gate only to hear St. Pete tell me, "Sorry, we do not seem to have your reservation." Was I predestined to miss every believer's eventual hope due to some theological small print on page 10,043?

That minister's assertion led me to really know what the Bible had to say about my eternal residence. After all, I remembered asking Jesus into my heart as a young boy and then attending church faithfully for years before finally responding positively to what I perceived to be God's voice calling me into full-time service for Him. I lived most of my life with the assurance that I did not need to worry about fire damage after I passed from this mortal coil. But how could I have the assurance that my early decision and eventual life's work were acceptable enough to provide confidence when I arrived at heaven's gate? Again, this is the *trust* part. I have to trust what God's Word clearly tells me. Romans 10:13 tells me that "Whosoever calls upon the name of the Lord shall be saved." I chose a long time ago to be in the "whosoever" camp.

In the matter of predestination, I offer a simple explanation as to God's dealing with mankind. I do not intend to write a doctrinal treatise on the subject, nor do I intend to boggle minds with new theological insight. We already have more than enough theology on the subject.

Let's begin with Romans 8:28 - NKJV

> *"And we know that all things work together for Good to those who love God, to those who are the called according to His purpose."*

This verse utilizes the word "the" prior to "called." The article "the" does not appear in the Greek text. The NIV renders the most accurate translation of this verse.

> *". . . those who love Him, who have been called according to His purpose."*

Everyone has been called. Not *everyone* will answer the call. Several truths help explain the mystery of predestination.

1. God's **Design** - to live in fellowship with mankind;
   From the very beginning of the world, God desired fellowship with His creation. Why would He create someone in His image only to view as little toys to be discarded when He was through with them? His fellowship proved to be the air that sustained their lives and gave them hope and dreams.

2. God's **Desire** - that all would be saved;
   God does not have a wasteful mentality. Everything He does is intentional and has redemption of mankind as its goal. Why *won't* everyone be saved? Is it really because God pre-programmed some to accept Him and others to reject Him? No. He gave man a free choice. Man is a free agent—free to choose his destiny. Only *His* quality of love could allow a man or woman to make the choice to willingly follow or freely reject the redemption contained in His love.

3. Man's **Choice** - to accept or reject Jesus Christ;
   Mankind makes the call either to accept God's gift of eternal life, or reject it all together. If we

reject Him, we choose to live in darkness. If we live in darkness, we cannot see His great plan for our lives. If we accept Him, we become predestined (foreordained) to be conformed to His plan. The point of predestination takes place after our choice. Once we choose, God says, "OK. *Now* I have a plan for your life."

4. God's **Plan** - Conformity to His Son Jesus Christ—based upon our choice;

> *"For whom He foreknew, he also predestined to be conformed to the image of His Son . . . "* (Romans 8:29)

God's Sovereignty and Man's Free Will

That simply means that before we can be conformed to Christ's image, we must get on the ship. Our positive choice sets us on a new course—a course for change. God begins the process that will conform us to Christ's attitudes about life. The next segments of life contain the lessons and illustrations of what that Christ-likeness really means and how our lives will take on meaning and purpose. From the moment of decision forward, it becomes God's will that we *trust* Him for what's ahead. If there is anything that is truly predestined from the beginning of time, it is that God presets certain *events*. Those involve participants by choice. Their will is not by-passed or annulled.

In his book, *Knowledge of the Holy*, A. W. Tozer tries to reconcile the seemingly contradictory beliefs of God's sovereignty and man's free will.

"An ocean liner leaves New York bound for Liverpool. Proper authorities have determined its destination. Nothing can change it. This is at least a faint picture of sovereignty. On board the liner are scores of passengers. These are *not in chains*; neither are their activities determined for them by some sort of decree. *They are completely free to move about as they will.* They eat, sleep, play, lounge about on the deck, read, talk, and so on. All the while the great liner is carrying them steadily toward a *predetermined* port. Both freedom and sovereignty are present here, and they do not contradict. So it is with man's freedom and the sovereignty of God." The mighty liner of God's sovereign design keeps its steady course over the sea of our life.

First Integrity Test

Now, back to Joseph. Potiphar noticed right away that Joseph was not the typical, run-of-the-mill slave and that he had a way of turning everything into gold. He was successful in all he did. This impressed Potiphar sufficiently to promote him to overseer of his whole house and all he owned. Joseph became overseer of the household staff, Potiphar's financial dealings, his agricultural interests, the whole nine yards! "All I want to concern myself with is what I eat. You take care of everything else. Handle it."

Joseph was devoted to God. The quality of his life was evident to Potiphar. He trusted Joseph in all things. Unprecedented favor had preceded Joseph from the time he was taken out of the pit and sold to the traders. He did not starve en route, nor did he arrive marred up from the cruel hands of over-bearing captors. He was at God's place in God's timeframe. But, things go from wonderful to terrible. The clear picture of Joseph's life suddenly blurred as Potiphar's wife noticed Joseph. She had too much time on her hands. During her idle moments, she began to fantasize what it would be like to sleep with Joseph. He's so young and virile! And handsome! So very handsome! She set about to seduce him. The seduction attempts fail time after time. Joseph reminded her of the trust her husband placed in him and that, while Joseph was overseer of all other facets of Potiphar's house, she was *off limits* to him.

A person can only take rejection for so long. She was used to getting her way. She was influential in her social circles because her husband was the captain of Pharaoh's personal bodyguards. Everybody knew him. She snapped her fingers and people responded. Not so with Joseph. He was determined to honor the trust of Potiphar and not sin against God. Only a heart that has been exposed to the transformational power of God's love can withstand the power of an enchantress promising ultimate and carnal bliss. After all, any man in his right mind could see the potential of such an opportunity. Any man, that is, except the man upon whom the favor of God rested and who was confident in the outcome of any situation as long as he let integrity guide his decisions.

Sinful Dalliance or Certain Dungeon?

What sets a healthy Christian apart from their worldly counterparts? They are aware of the process of being conformed to the image of Christ and determine to live in truth and walk in integrity. Accusations may be leveled at them but they know the truth and can live with whatever outcome it produces. Joseph found himself caught in an integrity trap. Either succumb to the yearnings of a prominent, socially elite "cougar" or remain steadfast in his faith and integrity and be willing to take whatever fallout it produced. To his way of thinking, even though he knew what was right, it was a no-win situation.

Mrs. Potiphar decided enough is enough! *Who is this slave to refuse her advances? Just who does he think he is, anyway?* She would not be made to feel foolish any longer. She'll show Joseph who has the real power. She's lonely. Given the Egyptian social structure, Potiphar was probably gone a lot and perhaps *even had other women*—as a man of his stature often indulged.

Victor Hugo said, "Hell hath no fury like a woman scorned." Maybe it was Potiphar's wife who gave him the inspiration for his famous statement. Her lust for Joseph shifted to self-preservation and she devised a plan in her own twisted mind. She waited for him to arrive at work. *Sin always waits for an occasion to happen.* Nobody else was in the house. As he entered, she grabbed him. How can he refuse her once she's in his arms? The fact is, he did refuse her and wiggled free from her grasp. In his haste he shed his coat and left it behind. Once again she was rejected. But, it's OK this time because she had her own plan. Holding his coat in her hand she cried, "Rape!" (39:14-15). I can hear her saying, "Enough of this! The die is cast. He could have had it all, but now, he'll pay!"

When Potiphar heard of the *alleged* attack on his wife, he was enraged and ordered Joseph into prison. Before Joseph knew it, he was packed off to prison—without even a word in his own defense. But, God did Joseph a favor. If the opportunity *had* presented itself for him to speak in his own defense, he probably would have. But he was rendered helpless. All he could do was keep his mouth shut and trust God. All he could see was the tapestry's backside, and it wasn't pretty. If he tried to say anything at all, he would look like a fool. He was a slave without social status or representation. *But God allowed this to happen with good reason.* It was so we can see what God can do if we will only take our hands off a situation we might think we need to control or defend.

Imagine how this scene *could* have played out. Joseph could have felt the pressure to comply with the whims of his employer's wife. He might even have enjoyed it. Just a perk of the job. If you can imagine that scenario taking place, you must also imagine the point in time when she gets what she wants, grows tired of it, and moves on to another hapless victim. Joseph could not plead his case before God because he was actually guilty and deserved to die at Potiphar's hands. The evil plan meant to capture one of God's elect young men would have ended justly. But Joseph did not fall into her trap. Yet, he still ended up in prison for being a person of integrity. The thought might have crossed his mind, "I know the truth and I can live with it."

In Dr. R. T. Kendall's book, *God Meant It For Good*, the familiar scenario of an accused child of God helps to clarify His dealings with us as His children. He says, "If you are a child of God and you have been hurt by being falsely accused, God feels more deeply about it than you do, but if you try to defend yourself, He will back off and say, 'Oh, you want to do it. That is what I wanted to do. So are you going to do it? Get on with it.'" If we will be quiet and not try to manipulate the situation, God will sovereignly deal with the situation at hand. He will vindicate His innocent children. That is why God did Joseph a favor by putting him in a position wherein he could say nothing. Sometimes it is a blessing when God shuts us up.

Some commentaries reveal that Potiphar was also the captain of the executioners. One word from him and Joseph would lose his head—literally. Other commentaries suggested that Potiphar *knew* what kind of a wife he had. Perhaps his anger was directed more at her than at Joseph. At any rate, the only social recourse, since Mrs. Potiphar had already blabbed news of the incident, was to throw Joseph into prison. Human life was a cheap commodity— often used solely for the entertainment of the wealthy. One might surmise that during the confrontation with Potiphar about his wife, Joseph's countenance must have conveyed a shocked reflection of innocence upon which Potiphar took notice. Yet, he *had* to do something in light of all the accusations and attention the incident had already garnered. Since Potiphar was also captain of the executioners, he was probably familiar with the keeper of the prison. Perhaps a kind word might have preceded Joseph into the bowels of the subterranean hell in which only the political outcasts and condemned took a forced residence.

(Verse 21)

> *"But the Lord was with Joseph and showed him mercy, and He gave him favor in the sight of the keeper of the prison."*

Verse 22 goes on to say that Joseph was made overseer of the prisoners. Again, Joseph prospered in all he did because he was a person of integrity. God knew his heart. *If God knows a man's heart, he can trust Him with his future.* Although this new position was not exactly a horizontal or vertical promotion, Joseph rose to the occasion as God further prepared him for a season of incredible influence and wisdom. At this very point in his life, Joseph lived purely by trusting that God knew what was ahead and that God would keep him safe.

Did you know that God could take evil and actually make it work for good? Did you know that He could turn lemons into lemonade if we let Him? Do you trust Him with your life? Even if we have stumbled and failed, there is forgiveness and restoration available through Him. We may not be able to change things in the past, but with His help we can make a significant change in our future.

Remember the three basic tenets of this narrative:

God has a plan. He knows what's ahead.
He's shaping a world-changer.

Doing Life in Real-Time:

1. Temptation is a constant of life.
   Regardless of who you are or what position you hold in your home, job, business or church, you *will* face temptation.

"No temptation has overtaken you except such as is common to man; but God is faithful, who will not allow you to be tempted beyond what you are able, but with the temptation will also make the way of escape, that you may be able to bear it." (1 Corinthians 10:13)

2. You may *fall* but you are not destined to *fail.*
The enemy of your soul constantly accuses you of being a loser and not having control of your mind. He shouts, "If you were a godly person, things like that would not enter your mind! You should be ashamed of yourself." He is a liar. He already lost the conflict of the ages.

Perhaps things in your life put you in a questionable light among your peers. Unfair accusations left you with a bitter spirit. Have you given it over to God? Have you let Him defend you? Maybe you gave into sexual temptation and know the destructive nature of such a choice. You'd give anything to have the opportunity to make the choice over again. This time, you'd chose differently. The truth is, now you can only influence your present and future—not your past. That belongs in the sea of God's forgetfulness—you know, the sea that has a "no fishing" sign on the shore.

Here's Your Handle:

When deceit and accusation become the enemy's weapons against you, remain steadfast in your integrity. God favors a man or woman whose heart is a place where integrity lives.

Prayer:

"Father, we understand so little about Your involvement in our lives. Help us to learn to trust You with our past, present and future. Give us the courage to reach out to You and surrender those things over which we have absolutely no control. Forgive us for striving. Forgive us for blaming You for our circumstances. Give us strength and courage to resist temptation and to live in integrity."

Chapter 3

"For Whom The Lord Loves . . ."

During our journey through life, I am convinced that God mandates the drive so we do not miss the vital discoveries and relationships long the way. He does not want us to experience life in "fly-by" mode. – J. Beaird

Joseph. Younger brother. Dreamer. Errand boy. Despised and conspired against. Sold and forgotten. Feared dead but actually far away. Hebrew slave in an Egyptian household. A person of integrity versus a lonely woman on the prowl. Falsely accused and imprisoned. Favored and functional.

Would you punish your children if they did everything right? That would not earn you points in the parent-of-the-year contest. Traditional parenting rightly recognizes the difference between affirmations for acceptable behavior and punishment for behavior beyond the boundaries of healthy childhood development. As parents, we want our children to become productive members of the communities in which they eventually reside. Consistency in loving discipline shapes the ensuing decisions our children will make as they each segue from one point in their personal development to another. The point is, we must help them distinguish between right and wrong behavior.

What about your job? What if you found a way to save your company lots of money—only to have to take a cut in pay or get demoted for it? Does that kind of reward system promote productivity and honesty? Most likely, not. If you knew the eventual outcome your discovery would have on your own wellbeing, you might not be prone to letting integrity guide your relationship with your boss or company for which you work. Rather, your efforts would gravitate toward the security of getting a regular paycheck for a bit longer—even if that meant your company would eventually go out of business. Not your problem.

If you were to speak with Joseph about the ups and downs of his young life, you might expect to hear him ask some tough questions about God's care and keeping—like, "Why am I being punished for doing everything right? I did not sin—even though everyone around me seemed bent on my demise. I only did what my father told me to do. I did not try to hurt anyone nor did I attack their character with my words. Even when my brothers threw me into the pit and then sold me into slavery, I did not cry out against them and accuse them with threats of getting even. Throughout the whole ordeal of being bound hand and foot, transported to a foreign country, displayed at the auction site for slaves, and eventually accused of something I had determined *not* to do, here I am in this musty cavern sharing space with foul-smelling, lice infested prisoners who do not seem to appreciate the truth about my innocence. My nice clothes must have been a give-away."

Joseph was being chastened by God *because* he did everything right. His chastisement, in situations we might not think merit His heavy hand, is always intentional and purposeful. He lovingly guides our steps and stops along unfamiliar paths on which we could easily take a wrong turn. In effect, we tend to interpret His guidance as punishment and not course correction. While His purpose is to get us from point A to point B without getting lost, the juncture at which we feel the pressure most acutely and abruptly along our path is His way of making sure we arrive at the place of His providence. He knows the way. We do not.

Psalm 103:9-10 says,

> *"He will not always accuse nor will He harbor his anger forever; He does not treat us as our sins deserve or repay us according to our iniquities. . . ."*

Verse 11 continues,

> *"For as high as the heavens are above the earth, so great is His love for those who fear Him; as far as the east is from the west, so far has He removed our transgressions from us."*

Chastisement Versus Punishment

It is not popular to consider reasons why our loving Father chooses to chasten us—especially if we've been faithful and walked in integrity. God does not chasten us to get even with us for sinning. He got even with sin when He sent His Son to the cross to defeat death, hell and the grave. When God chooses to chasten someone, it is that He might prepare that individual for something better, more valuable and more useful to His plan. We cannot conclude that all chastisement is punishment. In this scenario in which God consciously places his hand upon the life of Joseph, He does so to correct the course and prepare the servant for the final destination. Anything less would fall short of God's provision in the preservation of His chosen people.

Current sociological shifts from traditional to non-traditional values leave most people bereft of once commonly held beliefs about God, the relevance of the church, and issues of integrity. The moral compass that once pointed in a fixed direction now spins like a weathervane in a whirlwind. Is it any wonder that men and women face uncertainty in an age of shifting values and morphing belief systems? What was once wrong is now right and what was once right is now wrong. Yet, countless individuals accept the course corrections gained through God's chastisement and determine to be the people God can use. Perhaps His course corrections (chastisement) take the form of loss or pain—things that cause us to re-evaluate our present course of action. He lovingly uses situations and events to adjust our heading and discover again His route to the place of His providence. If our stated goal is to be used of Him, the present pain associated with course corrections will only be temporary and yield to a better understanding both of the tapestry of our life and the design He is weaving into it.

As D. L. Moody once sat on a platform, he heard the speaker make this statement: *"The world has yet to see what God can do with one man who is utterly committed to Him."* Mr. Moody said in his heart, "I propose to be that person." Within just a few days his church and house burned to the ground. History records D. L. Moody as one of the great men of God of all time. Yet, he was no stranger to difficulties as the loss of his home and church attest. Yet, through the course correction (chastisement) of the loving Father, Pastor Moody gained insight into God's providential plan and ultimate guidance toward his point of destiny.

One must understand the journey Moody took throughout his life. He did not attend school beyond the fifth grade. He was considered brash and crude and lived the young life of a street hoodlum. After he moved to Boston as a teenager, he was befriended by a Sunday School teacher in the Mt. Vernon Congregational Church (with whom he became lifelong friends). Having grown up in a

Unitarian family, young Dwight had never before heard the complete plan of salvation. He became passionate about reaching people who had never heard the incredible message of the Gospel of Jesus Christ. He eventually moved to Chicago and often wandered the streets looking for individuals to invite to a class wherein they could hear the same good news that had transformed his life. Conservative estimates vary, but Dwight L. Moody is believed to have introduced a million people to Christ. Given the fact he had never become an ordained minister, he knew his heavenly Father had a plan, He knew what was ahead, and He promised to keep him safe.

If God chooses to chasten you, and if you take it well, then you can be trusted. God's plan for Joseph and the vital role he would play in the preservation of both a heathen nation and those who were to become the Israelites was far greater than anything that could ever be seen at the time.

I need to give you the bad news. Living a godly life does not automatically guarantee that you will be recognized as being godly. When you consider how Joseph reacted properly and did not sin when faced with sexual temptation perpetrated by Mrs. Potiphar, you would expect God to vindicate him on the spot. But, He didn't—why? God had more in mind for His kingdom than Joseph's personal vindication.

Remember . . .

God has a plan. He knows what's ahead.
He's shaping a world-changer.

In his book, *God Meant it for Good*, R. T. Kendall dedicated a chapter to dealing with the topic of winning the battle but losing the war (p. 69). The Apostle Paul alludes to it as being "knocked down but not knocked out."

If we continue to take our vindication into our own hands, we may well win the battle at the expense of losing the war. At this precise juncture in God's dealing with his children, we must, at all costs, resist the temptation to take the situation out of God's hands and engage in self-vindication. That provides a short victory whose sweetness rapidly sours as God exposes self-serving, disobedient children who need another trip around the desert.

The Big Picture

God always has the "big picture" in mind when correcting our errant course. Only after He restores us to the trajectory capable of delivering us to our place of providence does He allow us to catch a glimpse of the tapestry. I said a *glimpse*—not the whole, but just enough to let us know *He knows* what He is doing and is capable of transforming ugliness into beauty.

Scripture does not mention whether or not Joseph was ever cleared of the charges trumped up by Potiphar's wife. As I mentioned in the last chapter, one look in Joseph's face told Potiphar all he needed to know about the truth of the situation. But, for Potiphar, a lot was on the line. He *had* to make an example of Joseph and maintain power over his subordinates. Our conjectures support Potiphar's "below the radar" recommendation to the keeper of the prison on Joseph's behalf. The trust he had for Joseph was lost on his wife. A man of his prominence probably knew of his wife's schemes from their sordid relational history. Perhaps theirs was a marriage with social implications in which they both lived behind a masked agenda. Quite possibly,

Potiphar's position was somehow linked to his wife's connections—either with family or social standing. At any rate, Joseph became the example warning others what happens when a slave gets out of line and ventures beyond the confines of his leash.

Joseph acted only with integrity and honor. Perhaps he did not know how to play the "game" others had played and won. But, he could live with himself and hold his head high, knowing he had not dishonored his God or his personal values. God used this time to adjust Joseph's course and prepare him for his personal place of providence. Point A to point B. Joseph was en route.

In his book, *Adversity Quotient: Turning Obstacles into Opportunities,* Paul Stoltz asserts, "Hope is the lifeblood of possibilities. You need not lose hope. You need not resign yourself to this 'fate.' You have the remainder of your life to make a difference, but only if you *refuse* to abandon the ascent" (p. 46). Joseph's rise through God's sovereign plan presented many opportunities to abandon the rise to the position God had prepared for him—even before his birth. But, Joseph stayed the course and reached deep within his soul to find the fortitude to resist personal and emotional defeat.

The Psalmist tells us, *"They hurt his feet with fetters (shackles), he was laid in irons (chained down). Until the time that his word came to pass, the word of the Lord tested him"* (105:18-19).

Joseph is a type of Christ. Jesus was never vindicated by those intent upon His death. When He rose from the dead, He didn't storm into Pilate's office and say, "See! I told you who I am but you wouldn't believe me." He did not feel the need to clear His name. Actually, only the believers saw Him after His death and resurrection. History would write His chronicles and validate His claims of divinity. He did not need to get ahead of what His Father planned in the redemption of all humankind. At that precise moment in history, He needed only to reassure the hearts of those who followed Him and who held to the hope of His claims.

He could easily have won the battle at the cross. He could have stopped the soldiers as they drove nails into His hands. A million angels could instantly appear and deliver Him from a cruel and painful death. But, He didn't want personal vindication. He had a greater love for His Father's whole kingdom.

As Kendall asserted, "He lost the battle so that He might win the war." A great cosmic court witnessed the events of His Passion as they played out in earth's arena. All of heaven watched as the Father's providence mandated the cruel and brutal death of His only son. No sane parent could ever stand by and refuse to lift a finger in defense of their only child. Adam had previously lost the legal claim to mankind when he chose to believe Satan rather than God. The moment for which all creation had waited now presented itself as the *only* opportunity to redeem fallen humankind. Jesus surrendered His physical life so He could descend into the presence of Satan and do battle in a spiritual venue. He lost the battle at Calvary, but won the war that determined ownership of the human race. He broke—once and for all time, Satan's claim on God's creation. By losing a battle, He placed Himself in position to win the war of the ages.

As we look at the injustices in Joseph's life, we must be aware that personal vindication would accomplish nothing for the kingdom of God. There are unseen reasons for continued suffering. If there were a more effective preparation than through trials or testing, God would use it. But—Father knows best. Knowing He will not put us through more than we can bear drives us to His side and assures us of His ability to keep us safe as long as we remain dependent on Him. Our position must be in close proximity to His loving heart. His protection covers us like an impenetrable shield, keeping deadly arrows from piercing our heart or inflicting irreparable harm.

Maybe it seems that God has denied your dreams time after time and you find yourself questioning His love. Your life did not follow the course in which you had your highest aspirations. Disappointment took residence in your heart and blocked out your ability to have dreams and hopes. You surrendered yourself to God, but He seems more intent upon your demise than your development. Wrap your mind around that thought.

Now, shift gears and allow Him to grant insight into your dilemma as He speaks to you from Hebrews 12:5-11.

"My son, do not despise the chastening of the Lord, nor be discouraged when you are rebuked by Him; (6) For whom the Lord loves He chastens, and scourges every son whom He receives. (7) If you endure chastening, God

deals with you as with sons; for what son is there whom a father does not chasten? (8) But if you are without chastening, of which you have all become partakers, then you are illegitimate and not sons. (9) Furthermore, we have had human fathers who corrected us and we paid them respect. Shall we not much more readily be in subjection to the Father of spirits and live? (10) For they indeed for a few days chastened us as seemed best to them, but He for our profit, that we may be partakers of His holiness. (11) Now no chastening seems to be joyful for the present, but painful; nevertheless, afterward it yields the peaceable fruit of righteousness to those who have been trained by it."

As I pointed out, we do not like to discuss chastening because we associate it with punishment. Personal preference avows that deliverance *from* a situation is more appealing than development *in* a situation. We do not understand what is at stake so we vie for the shortest, easiest route between two points. Years ago travel by automobile from state to state replaced travel by horse and buggy from town to town. Present day travel offers the widely accepted option to purchase a plane ticket and fly from state to state or country to country. We do not even consider driving from Florida to Iowa or somewhere else. Why? Because flying is the shortest and easiest distance between two points because we measure it in time instead of distance. The only apparent benefit of driving derives from being able to see the scenery, visit friends, or stop at a roadside fruit stand or gas station for a comfort break. The "fly-over" option eliminates scenic forays and new discoveries. During our journey through life, I am convinced that God mandates the drive so we do not miss the vital discoveries and relationships along the way. He does not want us to experience life in "fly-by" mode.

Perspective on Suffering and Testing

Two Greek words explain God's purpose on the topic of suffering in the life of the Christian. In his commentary, *Golden Nuggets from the Greek New Terstament*, Kenneth Wuest discusses the difference between the two words. They each mean "to test," but refer to different *kinds* of tests. It is important to know the difference because both sides of our nature is involved.

1. *Dokimazo* - the act of testing someone or something for the purpose of approving it (like a doctor taking his medical exams before he can practice medicine). The word has in it the idea of proving a thing whether it be worthy to be received or not.

2. *Peirazo* - to try or test intentionally with the purpose of discovering what good or evil, what power or weakness was in a person or thing. Putting to test with the intention and hope of breakdown (car testing and product safety).

Dokimazo is generally used of God, but never of Satan. Satan *never* puts to the test in order that he might approve. By the same token, Satan always exploits our points of weakness. His plan reflects a desire to dismantle a believer's confidence and destroy their faith. Joseph underwent the *dokimazo* tests for the purpose of God's approval and use. God had a plan. He knew what was ahead. God had plans for His chosen people that required someone with the right character to endure the "field testing" necessary to prepare them for the ultimate position of prominence and influence.

Inevitable testing fuels development and

dependence upon God. The road of life contains detours from preconceived plans and generally reveals needed lessons on becoming useful to the Father's intended agenda. The child of God often experiences unexpected turns in life's road. As they learn to depend on a heavenly Father who continually proves His love, they eventually navigate the turns with skill and confidence.

Doing Life in Real Time:

1. You must not allow bitterness to drive its strong root deep into your vulnerable soul.

   Are you bitter because someone treated you unjustly? God says, *"Get rid of all bitterness, rage and anger, brawling and slander, along with every form of malice. Be kind and compassionate to one another, forgiving each other, just as in Christ God forgave you."* Ephesians 4:31-32

2. You must not allow bitterness to become the filter through which you see and discern God's presence in your life. Rather, surrender to Him during the onset of your trial and trust Him for the best.

   Has your bitterness been turned toward God? He

says, *"And we know that in all things God works for the good of those who love Him, who have been called according to his purpose . . Who shall separate us from the love of Christ? Shall trouble or hardship or persecution or famine or nakedness or danger or sword? . . . . No, in all these things we are more than conquerors through Him who loved us."* Romans 8:28,35,37

3. You must not seek self-vindication. God promised to vindicate you once the process is in motion.

   Have you become vengeful and vindictive toward those who have mistreated you? God says, *"Do not repay anyone evil for evil . . . Do not take revenge, my friends, but leave room for God's wrath, for it is written: 'It is mine to avenge; I will repay,' says the Lord . . . Do not be overcome by evil, but overcome evil with good."* Romans 12:17,19,21

If you find yourself in a situation in which you experience discomfort or pain, realize that God can bless you right where you are. These can be the most joyous days ever! After all, who knows what God can do with you if you are completely yielded to Him right where you are? Don't be too hasty to change things. You don't know what's at stake. Do not focus on the present battle. Focus on the entirety of the war. It is better to win the war. Realize that your present involvement in the pain or discomfort you feel is necessary for God to be able to utilize the gifts He's given you and to develop them fully.

Here's Your Handle:

Bitterness only serves the enemy of your soul. He uses it to choke spiritual vitality from you. Determine to say "no" to vindictive thoughts and imaginations. Doing so allows God to infuse you with His presence.

Chapter 4

Right Man, Right Place, Right Time

"Preparation is not so painful when you consciously choose it, but what makes it hard is when you don't recognize it for what it is." - *R. T. Kendall*

Our very nature demands that we know where we're going, what's ahead, and what we can count upon to come to pass. We make plans and get irritated if someone else plans an event for us without consulting us first—that is, of course unless someone dear to us planned a surprise party in our honor. That trumps all feelings of indignation. But when someone actually pulls you into his or her dilemma, your feelings of frustration and resentment take on a credibility whose origin traces back to an already bad attitude. Most plans orchestrated by others lack sufficient foreknowledge to avert probable embarrassment.

You might say that God had an extraordinary plan for Joseph that involved some extraordinary preparation. God's plan involved more than a drama involving a single individual. His plan called for unprecedented and elaborate measures to prepare His chosen subject for the task ahead. It called for precise timing and intricate script writing. It mandated that His star player follow the lines exactly and never wander outside the storyline.

It might be a good idea to discuss the whole premise upon which a plan is brought about in the life of a believer. It is likely fair to say that most people do not appreciate getting sucked into someone else's plan—especially if it involves time and resources originally allotted elsewhere. And, chances are good that the time and resource now being tapped was the product of planning and anticipation. The imaginations about the finished product that had once abounded now evaporated like water on a hot sidewalk. Getting roped into someone else's plan becomes the newest saga of disappointment to be shared, of course, at a much later time. Just go along with it and hope you can salvage some of your day. "Be flexible," you think, as you begin to wonder when was the last time someone was flexible enough to accommodate *your* plans.

While personal plans often fall prey to events originating outside of an individual's list of personal expectations and preferences, they still have their own trajectory—even if it has been altered by the intersection with other agendas. In a perfect world, personal plans triumph and bring notoriety to the person capable of staying on course until the task's completion. However, we do not live in a perfect world. We seem beset by a myriad of complications that have somehow woven their threads into our tapestry.

Comedy of Errors

Say, for instance, you have your Saturday all planned. What you really want is a day when nobody can access you. You begin your day early to make the most of your time alone. You have a few little jobs to do around the house. You discover you need a certain tool you don't have but your friend does. So, you call him and get permission to borrow the tool. While on the phone, he relates to you that his wife has been gone for a few days to visit relatives. He told her that he was going fishing, but actually planned to surprise her by painting the living room. After you arrive at his home, you step inside while he gets the tool. He returns with the tool and says, "Say, while you are here, could you help me move this bookcase out from the wall so I can paint behind it?" You say, "Sure." After all, he's loaning you a tool. You can be helpful.

While moving the bookcase, you notice a vase on the second shelf filled with a colored liquid. You both ignore it as you'll only be moving the shelf a couple of feet at the most. He'll quickly paint behind the shelf, you'll help him move it back, and you'll be on your way—five minutes max. At one foot of a two-foot move, the vase falls over and deposits its colorful contents on the carpet (which, I might add, just happens to be a light shade of tan). Your friend mutters an expletive. You *think* the same word. He runs into the kitchen and grabs the first absorbent material he can grab—the ornamental tea towel hanging on the oven door handle. Moments later, the new spot in the rug claims its first victim—a similarly spotted tea towel. You watch as your friend continues to sop up the liquid. You are not sure, but you think the tea towel reached its maximum absorbency a while ago. Finally, it seems to be all sopped up, except for that interestingly new spot right in front of the bookshelf.

"What now?" he asks you. He looks in vain for a spot remover. No luck. "I'm really sorry," he says as he darts for the door. "Maybe the hardware store has something. The paint roller is right there in the tray beside the bookcase. I'll just be a minute. Could you paint behind the shelf and we'll move the case back into place in a few minutes." At this point, what can you do? You say OK, and decide to help the poor guy out. As you pick the roller up, you notice a series of large nail holes and wall blemishes right behind the bookcase. A job for spackling compound. You look around for some. None. Your friend has already left. You know another guy in the same neighborhood who might have some. You call him. He does.

As you arrive at his house, you briefly explain the circumstances and leave. At this point, things seem redeemable. You can still have the wall painted before he gets back. Since he will need to get back into the garage, you park in the street, about a half block away in the first available spot.

As you try to get back into the house, you discover the door is locked. Things are now starting to get complicated. The tool you came to borrow is inside on the table. Your friend still isn't back. You check the other doors, only to find them locked also. Then, you notice the dining room window is open— evidently for fresh air while painting. There is only one little problem. The window is about six feet off the ground. So . . . you pull the picnic table over to the window, stand on it so you can reach the window and solve your problem.

A neighbor has silently been watching your manner of problem solving and, not knowing who you are, assumes the worst and calls the police. There is an almost immediate response from a patrolman just two streets over. When you are about half way into the window, you notice the tool on the table and the bookcase across the room. Suddenly you feel a firm grip on your ankle. "Come down from there, slowly!"

As you comply, you suddenly realize things are now getting very complicated. You try to explain the situation to the officer who doesn't tell you he's already been investigating a series of burglaries in the same area. Handcuffs and frisk. Not only have things gotten complicated, now they've gotten humiliating as well.

When things just couldn't get any worse, your friend's wife pulls into the driveway. You've never met her because you work with her husband. You figure it's his wife and inadvertently mutter, "Oh no. She's home early." The officer hears you and assumes he has his man. She gets out of her car and looks curiously at the cruiser then at you and the officer standing there on the driveway. Since she has never met you, she asks what's going on. The officer tells her that he caught you trying to slip into her house—probably to rob her!

Your efforts to explain only fall on deaf ears. She mentions that her husband told her that he'd be at the lake fishing. As the officer is about to place you in the back seat of his cruiser, your friend pulls into the driveway. Thirty minutes later, you're on your way. Your job at home will now have to wait. The tool you came to borrow is still on your friend's table.

Have you ever had a day like that? Just when you think things can't get more complicated, they do. A Christian should have a different insight into complicated circumstances. We don't have to *understand* the process if we'll only *recognize* the product. Usually, all we have to focus upon is the process—which, I might add, is usually uncomfortable. It is the process that eliminates potential champions. For that reason, not everyone becomes a champion.

Chapter 40 finds Joseph in prison. Last chapter, I shared how Psalm 105:18 revealed how he was put in shackles and irons. The lesson was about chastening. The application centered on our desire for vindication in the midst of unfair accusation. Remember, God doesn't chasten us to get back at us for sin in our life. He got back at sin at the cross. Only the enemy of your soul uses that tactic. He employs any and all means to demean you, de-value you, and get you to believe that God is not pleased with you as a person or as one of His children. He continually bombards you with thought bombs— trying to destroy confidence you need in the forward progress of your walk with Christ. He accuses you of your already fragile sense of righteousness and exploits your vulnerability. He wants to leave you shell shocked—not knowing whether or not you will survive the battlefield he's created in your mind. His goal is to dissuade you from pursuing fellowship with the Father and eroding any trust you might have had in Him.

Two New Dreamers

Now, it appears that Joseph gets two new cellmates. Verse 1 tells us that the butler and the baker of the king of Egypt offended him somehow and ended up in prison. The average individual knows little about imprisonment simply for the crime of offending someone. Yet, both men—in the household of the king, succeeded at crossing the line and were both banished to the darker corners of the building's basement. While we might consider this an unrelated incident, the presence of these two men provided an essential link between Joseph and his eleven brothers back in Canaan. Both his brothers and his new cellmates figured into dreams he either had or would be called upon to interpret. All parties concerned became strands God intended to weave into the beautiful masterpiece of Joseph's personal tapestry. God does everything according to the creative design in His mind. He paints that design upon the beauty of the earth He created and upon the lives He wants desperately to redeem.

The butler and the baker had troubling dreams. The usual thing to do was to consult an interpreter—someone in the "black-magic" arts like an astrologer or soothsayer. Their culture provided for practitioners who claimed to see beyond the natural world into the supernatural world. Some gained their abilities from Satan and some were just "wannabes" intent on gaining notoriety through their hopeful association with the real deal. At any rate, consultation with these seers was usually limited to people who had power and influence. They walked a fine line between keeping their heads attached to their shoulders and formulating policy by advising the king. Their counsel guided those who ruled countries and kingdoms and their services were generally not available to people of lesser social and economic footing. This group certainly included those incarcerated for offending the people upstairs.

Commentary reveals the distinct possibility of this pair of dreams occurring after about a year in prison. That means they most likely knew Joseph and had become familiar enough with each other to discern when something was wrong. The fear of uncertainty emanated from inside their hearts and minds and manifested outwardly through their countenance—revealing that all was not at peace within. When he asked them what was wrong, they told him of their discomforting dreams and further related their frustrations with not knowing their meanings. Everyone has dreams. But these dreams had that certain captivating feature capable of instilling a sense of ominous danger associated with the fear of not being able to detect their own survival in the matter. Perhaps, the graphic nature of their dreams literally imprinted upon their conscious minds the dreadful possibilities, which might become deadly probabilities.

Earlier in this book, we called Joseph a dreamer. He too, had unusual dreams. Little did he know then or even now that God had given him a special gift—specializing in dreams. Now, it appears that he can use this special gift again, except now God will give him the interpretation of someone else's dreams. Perhaps now he would begin to understand that God desires to use him in a manner he could never have imagined. Perhaps now he started seeing the bigger picture of the tapestry God was weaving of his life's purpose. He began to emerge as the leader God meticulously prepared for a time yet to come but would play an unprecedented role in the preservation of God's people.

The following scenario played out that night in the depths of the prison.

Butler:

A vine with three branches; it budded and provided grapes which he squeezed into Pharaoh's cup, then placed the cup back into Pharaoh's hand.

Baker:

Three white baskets on his head; the top basket had baked goods for Pharaoh but the birds came and ate them.

Joseph's interpretation:

Butler:

Three branches are three days; after three days Pharaoh will restore him to his position. Pretty straightforward. Not too much about which to get upset.

Baker:

After three days, Pharaoh will execute him and hang him where the birds can pick at his body. Pretty blunt. Looks like he drew the short straw.

After his interpretation of the butler's dream, Joseph added, "When you get back into your position, put in a good word for me. I want to get out of here!" But the last verse of chapter 40 and the 1st verse of chapter 41 reveal that the butler "forgot" Joseph and he stayed in prison for another 2 years. God saw that Joseph—though innocent and ignorant of God's processes, tried to abrogate what God put into place in the character and spiritual formation of a man destined for greatness and shaped for a special purpose. When God puts us in a particular place, He doesn't want us to try to manipulate the situation. As Joseph must have felt like he couldn't take any more injustice, God was saying, "You can, and you must. I need to bring something in you to the surface that no simple trial could cause to emerge. While you do not know my purpose, the product will astound you! Sit tight. Be patient. Let me do what is necessary so that my work can be perfected in uniting the divine with the human elements I chose to alter the course of human history."

Not Quite Yet, Joseph . . .

Joseph tried to nudge the hand of providence and help God design his tapestry, but the timing was wrong. Perhaps the greatest hindrance to God's refining process is when we reach out of the frying pan to try to turn the temperature down. Joseph was not responsible for what happened to the butler and the baker. He was simply there, and, through the revelation of God's Spirit to his, they were simply given advance notice of what was to happen. The event's foreknowledge signaled a freedom promise for one and a death sentence for the other. I often wonder why one had to die while the other was able to resume his life of servitude in the king's court. Yet, God desired to punctuate the occasion in the butler's mind in such a way that he could never really forget the event or the young man who foretold it. God does not waste anything in His intervention of human history. Every event is a strand He carefully weaves into just the right place at just the right time.

Joseph emerges again as a fore-shadowing (or type) of Christ. While it was not his interpretation that caused one to be restored and the other to be executed, so it is with Jesus Christ. It was not His coming that sent anybody to hell. He came to provide a way for mankind to gain opportunity to avoid hell. John 3:17 says, *"For God sent not His Son into the world to condemn the world, but that the world through Him might be saved."*

Jesus never says no. It is His coming that saves people. The only time He will ever say no will be at the final judgment when all stand before Him and some find it is too late to change their minds and make a decision to follow Christ into Heaven's reward. He may have to say to you, *"I never knew you: depart from Me you worker of iniquity!"* (Matt. 7:23) You may cry out for a second chance since you will then know how you failed. But, the Bible says in Matt. 22:13 that Jesus will give you no mercy as He says, *"Bind him hand and foot, and take him away, and cast him into utter darkness."* Jesus has given you chance after chance to accept Him. You can never blame Jesus if you end up in hell. He gave you endless opportunities to accept His grace and allow Him to cleanse your sins and erase your past.

Look again at verse 1 of chapter 41:

" . . . *at the end of two full years* . . . "

Joseph had asked the butler to put in a good word for him. Evidently, he did not because word never came. Since the butler was in charge of Pharaoh's personal matters, it was necessary for Pharaoh to perceive him as discreet and discerning. For him to put in a good word for a convict just didn't coincide with his newly regained favor. *Take care of number one. Do nothing to arouse suspicion. Do everything to curry favor! Become indispensable to him because he has the power with his spoken word to banish you once again—perhaps to the same fate as your old friend, the baker.*

Now, two full years had passed. To say that, 'time flies when you are having fun,' simply does not apply here. In fact, time crawled along at a snail's pace since the butler had been restored to his former position. Perhaps a day came when Joseph simply stopped listening for sounds of approaching footsteps en route to his cell to liberate him from his forced residency within the bowels of the prison. If we could reflect upon Joseph's situation for a minute, we'd see that he probably missed his family and just wanted to go home. At this point, it had been over eleven years since he'd seen his father—to whom he had been very close. But nothing positive seemed to be happening as he watched one day fade into another, then another, then another.

The Providential Hand of God

Now, the hand of Providence begins again to move. God's hand moves back and forth, inserting one strand of a particular texture and color then another and another in the tapestry He is creating for a special *purpose* in a special *life*. The saga of Joseph's unfortunate twist of fate begins to emerge as a discernable pattern—not entirely clear, but partially perceptible. The events associated with the life of the young daddy's boy begin to take shape exactly in the timeframe the Father had in mind.

In a nutshell, Pharaoh had two dreams.

First Dream:
> Seven fat cows came up out of the river;
> Seven skinny cows came up out of the same river and ate the seven fat cows.

Second Dream:
> Seven heads of grain came up on one stalk;
> Seven thin heads came up on the same stalk and devoured the plump heads of grain.

Needless to say, Pharaoh was troubled and called for his interpreters. Nobody could interpret his dreams. Either they did not understand the severity of the request or they did not feel threatened by their own failure to give the interpretation. In both dreams there was a set of sevens followed by a second set of sevens. His first dream involved a pastoral setting and the second dream involved an agricultural setting. Surely, *someone* could find some discernable meaning in dreams with numbers that reoccurred in such dramatic fashion. One involved crops and the other involved flocks. No other country in the world had such an elaborate infrastructure as Egypt and these two settings represented its lifeblood. The nature of the dreams was such that Pharaoh could not simply dismiss them as a product of his own subconscious worry or reaction to food he had eaten late in the day. The dreams truly troubled him. He *knew* instinctively that they held meaning beyond the ordinary palace business of running his kingdom. The seers could not find significance in the dreams. God withheld the meaning from them because He had a plan to elevate a very special convict.

There's an interesting observation in verse 9. The butler said, "Now I know I've messed up in the past, but I know a guy I met in prison who has a way of hitting the nail right on the head when it comes to dreams. I think he could help." Wow. He had remained silent about Joseph for two years and now offers a solution that could land him right back in the prison—or *worse.*

Pharaoh called for Joseph. *Finally,* he heard the footsteps of destiny approaching his cell. He heard the key insert into the lock and the clicking of the lock's tumblers signal providential opportunity. "Pharaoh wants to talk," the jailer told him.

After making himself presentable for the king's court, Joseph entered the great hall wherein Pharaoh and his company had gathered. If I were a betting man, I'd bet that none of the seers were too excited to see him arrive. Anyone else in the hall must have thought about his convict status and mentally questioned the reason for his visit. Yet, Pharaoh himself had called for his presence and that was all they needed to know for now. Perhaps they were curious about the report the butler gave and wanted to watch as the jailbird crashed and burned right in front of them all. This was the moment God had woven into his tapestry. This was the design He meticulously produced through the myriads of trials and hardships His young protégé had endured. Center stage! Center moment! Center purpose! Joseph recognized the providential intersection with his jail time and wanted to give credit where credit was due.

He began, *"I cannot do it, but God will give Pharaoh*

the answer . . . " (41:16). Impressed with his humility and non-assuming demeanor, he decided he could trust Joseph and proceeded to relate his two dreams. The young man seemed unfazed as he listened to the explanation, Pharaoh's apparent bewilderment, and the report about the seers' failure to give meaning to the dream. Joseph gained the attention of everyone in the hall as he gave an instant interpretation. *"The dreams are one and the same* . . . " (41:25). There would be seven years of abundance followed by seven years of famine. Pharaoh allowed the ominous words to sink in as he listened to the young man intent on giving more credit to God than to himself. He discerned that Joseph was not intent on establishing his own reputation nor did he cheaptalk Pharaoh's in-house council. He simply spoke as God gave him the understanding of the pending turn in the national economy. Most Egyptians had never known a time when food and water were scarce. They had only known Egypt as the crown jewel of the world in terms of commerce and commodity.

God prepared Pharaoh's mind and heart for this very moment in which Joseph rendered the accurate but unpopular interpretation. Only God can change a man's heart to be receptive to something he normally might consider outlandish or extreme. Once God reveals His plan, no earthly force can resist the forward progress of a plan whose origin is from the heart of the Father. Since God prepared Pharaoh to be able to receive a truthful account of Egypt's future dilemma, He also prepared him to receive a viable option in getting through the next fourteen years. Joseph was wise enough to know that God had a plan. Now, he rightly discerned that this was the plan God designed all along. This was the reason why his life had taken on such a painfully slow pace and required he go through everything he once questioned. Because of that knowledge, he bravely made a suggestion.

The Tapestry: A Glimpse of God's Plan

First of all, he told Pharaoh that he needed to select a wise and discerning man to oversee the plan. His suggestion involved stewardship over the land for seven years by planning ahead for the famine and establishing storage areas in which crops would be stored. Again, Pharaoh listened as Joseph spoke. He also listened for the suggestion that Joseph be considered as a player in the solution to what lay ahead. That suggestion never came from Joseph. He did not promote himself because he already learned not to abrogate the plan of God with his own preferences. God was at work in Pharaoh's heart and mind as he was drawn to Joseph's wisdom. Since

Joseph clarified God as being the source of the plan, Pharaoh did not feel threatened by an ambitious Joseph. God made it clear to Joseph while he was interpreting Pharaoh's dreams, that he would be appointed to oversee the next fourteen years of stewardship in the land.

God has a plan. He knows what's ahead.
He's shaping a world-changer.

In his book, *Joseph: Overcoming Obstacles Through Faithfulness*, in reference to the pain of patience, Gene Getz lists 4 principles by which to live:

Principle 1:

> Learning to wait patiently strengthens our confidence in God without reducing the self-confidence we need to function in life. (James 1:2-4)
>
> *"My brethren, count it all joy when you fall into various trials, knowing that the testing of your faith produces patience. But let patience have its perfect work, that you may be perfect and complete, lacking nothing."*

Principle 2:

> A period of waiting often allows time for us to develop true character and to reflect that character to others. (Rom. 5:3-4)

"And not only that, but we also glory in tribulations, knowing that tribulation produces perseverance: and perseverance, character; and character, hope."

Principle 3:

A period of waiting often creates opportunities for advancement that may not happen otherwise. (Romans 8:28)

"And we know that all things work together for good to those who love God, to those who are called according to His purpose."

Principle 4:

A period of difficulty and pain helps us develop wisdom we otherwise might not have. (2 Cor. 1:6-7)

"For if we are afflicted, it is for your consolation and salvation, which is effective for enduring the same sufferings which we also suffer. Or if we are comforted, it is for your consolation and salvation. And our hope for you is steadfast because we know that as you are partakers, so also you will partake of the consolation."

It's the same way with our Christian lives. If we can come to view adversity, false accusations and false treatment as opportunities for growth, we'll develop wisdom and judgment beyond our years. A man or woman does not simply decide one day to become a soldier and travel somewhere to engage the enemy. He or she enlists in a painful process designed to turn normal individuals into fighting machines capable of combat and certain of victory. Their time in boot camp prepares them for what they might face on the battlefield as they become one with their weapons. Pain and perseverance transforms them into soldiers capable of hearing their commander as he issues the order to advance.

Throughout my forty-plus years of active ministry, pain and disappointment often accompanied the process of establishing a new church or reaching a community for Christ. Personal agenda could not exist alongside the Father's agenda. Now, looking back, I understand how each painful lesson prepared me for what God had in mind when He called me into His service and how I needed to shed any semblance of my old self. God's will always requires obedience and submission. He cannot use our self-will until He refines it and it becomes a reflection of our will to persevere in the venue in which He's placed us.

In her book, *Tramp for the Lord*, Corrie ten Boom discussed her feelings about her release from a Nazi concentration camp. There is a common thread that links her life to Joseph's.

"When you are dying—when you stand at the gate of eternity—you see things from a different perspective than when you think you may live for a long time. I had been standing at that gate for many months, living in Barracks 28 in the shadow of the crematorium. Every time I saw the smoke pouring from the hideous smokestacks I knew it was the last remains of some poor woman who had been with me in Ravensbruck. Often I asked myself, "When will it be my time to be killed or die?"

But I was not afraid. Following Betsie's death, God's presence was even more real. Even though I was looking into the valley of the shadow of death, I was not afraid. It is here that Jesus comes the closest, taking our hand, and leading us through.

One week before the order came to kill all the women of my age, I was free. I still do not understand all the details of my release from Ravensbruck. All I know is, it was a miracle of God. I stood in the prison yard—waiting the final order. Beyond the walls with their strands of barbed wire stood the silent trees of the German forest, looking so much like the gray-green sets on the back of one of our theater stages in Holland.

Mimi, one of the fellow prisoners, came within whispering distance. "Tiny died this morning," she said without looking at me. "And Marie also."

Tiny! "Oh Lord, thank You for letting me point her to Jesus who has now ushered her safely into Your presence." And Marie. I knew her well. She lived in my barracks and had attended my Bible talks. Like Tiny, Marie had also accepted Jesus as her Lord. I looked at the long rows of Barracks. "Lord, if it was only for Tiny and Marie—that they might come to know You before they died—then it was all worthwhile."

A guard spoke harshly, telling Mimi to leave the yard. Then he said to me, "Face the gate. Do not turn around."

The gate swung open and I glimpsed the lake in front of the camp. I could smell freedom.

"Follow me," a young girl in an officer's uniform said to me. I walked slowly through the gate, never looking back. Behind me I heard the hinges squeak as the gate swung shut. I was free, and flooding through my mind were the words of Jesus to the church at Philadelphia: "Behold, I have set before thee an open door, and no man can shut it . ."

Doing Life in Real Time:

1. Your timetable does not always coincide with God's. You live life in the context of seventy or eighty years and God has always existed.

2. God's timetable includes the rearrangement of your life perspective. He seeks to deliver you from the grind of unfruitful activities and misplaced priorities. Your agenda no longer gets center stage.

3. God's timetable is always precise and purpose-driven. When He enacts a plan, He moves forward in resourceful partnership with individuals intent on pleasing Him.

I realize the difficulty in applying principles like I've outlined while you're in the midst of the ordeal. That's not the application I want to make. Understand that. Your understanding of God's desire to develop you must actually begin before the trial. Things may be fine for you right now. Thank

God if that's the case. However, in this age of uncertainty, nothing is certain. Your ability to face whatever is ahead must begin right now with the absolute confidence that your life belongs to Him.

Until you possess that confidence, you will struggle with God's plan. Until you give your life over to Him, you'll fear what's ahead. Remember . . .

God has a plan. He knows what's ahead.
He's shaping a world-changer.

Here's Your Handle:

God is never late. You may not appreciate the time you are required to wait for God to provide what you prayed for, but He has a timing pattern to the tapestry He's weaving for your life.
It's a masterpiece!

Chapter 5

The Providential Timetable

The effectiveness of God's plan begins the moment an individual relinquishes control to Him and surrenders any pre-conceived notion of how their personal development should take place. — *J. Beaird*

Seeds. Useless until someone places them in the earth and allows the process of nurture and nature to help them become more than just a nugget of indistinguishable matter. But, it takes time. The process of growth is essential. There is one thing God will not do and that is to make things happen quicker than the appointed time. In His own wisdom, He has chosen to be bound by time. Eccl. 3:11 says, *"He has made everything beautiful in His time."*

As a minster for over forty years, I always enjoyed performing marriages. (It's *one* time everybody listens to you.) I required a time of counseling prior to agreeing to marry the couple because I felt that if I'm involved in the preparation process, and give the couple some good tools to use in their new beginning together, then I can know I've done everything possible as a pastor in helping this new couple begin their lives together. I can put my stamp of approval upon their union because I know they're taking the preparation seriously. If a couple would not agree to the counseling, I would not perform the ceremony. The day arrives when the bride walks down the aisle in her beautiful dress and veil and their big day is at hand.

There is a vital spiritual principle here. When God's providential plan unfolds in our lives, we will gain an understanding of the process. The other side of that statement reveals that if the entirety of God's providential plan has *not* unfolded in our lives, our understanding of the process remains incomplete. That simply means He has more to do in lives in which He chose to fulfill certain destinies.

If you are a Jeff Foxworthy fan, you most likely know you're a redneck, "If your idea of a 7 course meal is a bucket of KFC and a six-pack." He usually paints a picture of people capable of enjoying the simple things in life without being affected by how others perceive them. The people whom he openly converses and jokes about have several indicators that reveal their social status and preferential lifestyle. Likewise, if you've trusted your life into the keeping and guidance of the Lord, you'll know God's providential plan is about to emerge when several indicators reveal instances of self-discovery in which you discern the hand of the Master Weaver. You will know God's providential plan is in play when . . .

You have nothing left of yourself. You border on exhaustion because you felt all the investment of effort, time and resources needed to originate with you. If you respond and say, "I cannot see my way out of this. I don't understand where this is going," then you know God's timetable remains indiscernible and His process only comes to fruition as He introduces more strands of color and texture to the tapestry being woven—yours. This is the precise time when you realize you are helpless.

Earlier in my ministry I came to a point of complete helplessness. I could not write another word to another sermon. I did not want to talk to people or be around them. I did not want to be bothered with their concerns. My well was dry. Convinced that God had abandoned me, I ceased trying to get close to a God who seemed so far away as the totality of my strength ebbed. It was *then* that God's providential plan lifted a broken servant to gain at least a partial understanding of the process in which God desired to create something truly wonderful. The lesson I learned from the years of struggle and discomfort revealed something about God I never learned in seminary. He *never* leaves his children without hope and He *always* provides for them—especially during the times of spiritual formation in which they come to trust His hand and anticipate His finished product in their lives. Not only does God seek to build us, but He also seeks to earn our trust. The process becomes the two sides of a well-nurtured relationship in which trust trumps everything else. He simply wants the satisfaction of knowing we trust Him.

Second, *God's providential plan includes external elements that did not originate within our personal scheme machine.* God's plan unfolded when an event appeared for which there was no natural explanation. He took the emerging scenario out of man's hand and created a need to consider the supernatural aspects of His unfolding and prophetic revelation. He did not trust the seers in the palace of Pharaoh because their power came from Satan. Rather, He used the king's unsettling dreams to summon His servant from the depths of the dungeon chambers and provide a platform upon which to proclaim His intent for that region.

Humankind sees things on a finite level. God sees events in the larger context of world history. His plans—even for a single individual, have been in motion since before that individual ever acknowledged His presence or considered His sovereignty. He told the prophet Jeremiah, "Before I formed you in the womb I knew you. Before you were born, I sanctified you," (1:5). We cannot gain heavenly perspective from a finite and myopic point of reference.

Third, *God's providential plan fills in the gaps of human experience.* When the common explanation fails to provide necessary answers, God's plan is afoot. When all human efforts fall short, God does His best work. He waits for us to realize the deficit of our individual and collective wisdom, and then He creates a scenario capable of revealing His ultimate control over every event of every human in the entire world. Human experience can only provide viable answers for very little of what humankind faces with each new day and each new challenge. To be certain, God *did* create mankind with the innate ability to think, solve problems, and arrive at proven operating procedures linked to recurrent tasks or problem sets. But, God also created mankind with a curiosity about the supernatural realm in which *only He* has an established operating procedure and *only*

He knows the outcome. Human willingness to consider something outside the realm of their collective knowledge base provides God with the opportunity both to display His handiwork and demonstrate His providence.

Fourth, *God's providential plan isolates and identifies the point at which we claim control.* From that point on, He lovingly changes the trajectory of our intentions from pleasing self to pleasing Him. He shows us that once we give Him control of our lives, He takes us seriously. Our plans fall short and do not incorporate the entirety of the beautiful plan He's weaving into our tapestry. He shows us that anything we do to emancipate ourselves from the weaver's loom only leaves us in a tangled mess of our own making. Joseph figured he had an ace up his sleeve with the butler's emancipation and restoration to position. He was wrong. He tried to manipulate the situation. He tried to anticipate God's timing. Remember! God wants to make everything beautiful *in His time.* Joseph undoubtedly had discerned that others began looking to him for guidance and answers while residing among society's outcasts. The situation resembled the lyrics to "Hotel California" by the early 70's rock group, the Eagles, penned by songwriters, Glenn Frey, Don Henley, and Don Felder. The final verse gives the bottom line for those unfortunate enough to have "checked in" to the hotel during their search for an illusive, yet immoral fulfillment.

> "Last thing I remember, I was
> Running for the door
> I had to find the passage back to the
> place I was before;
> 'Relax' said the night man,
> 'We are programmed to receive.
> You can check out any time you like,
> But you just can never leave!"

The prison provided no natural way of escape other than to take one's own life. He could have "checked out" but he could not leave. Joseph had not embarked on a personal journey to find fulfillment, erotic quest, or fame and fortune. His only infraction was to live a life of integrity and chastity while the world around him maintained its narcissistic orbit.

The butler "remembered" Joseph's dream. It would now be good for the butler, good for Joseph, and good for Pharaoh. But until this time, God kept it out of Joseph's hands. Are you afraid that God will forget where you are? God reached for Joseph. Gen. 41:14 reveals, 'Pharaoh sent and called Joseph, and they brought him *hastily* out of the dungeon." He knows exactly where you are and the precise time in which you think *you* are in control. The effectiveness of God's plan begins the moment an individual relinquishes control to Him and surrenders any preconceived notion of how their personal development should take place. The good news of the Gospel proclaims you may be saved when you come to the end of your own strength. He's reaching for you because His plan is to elevate you to a place of prominence only He can ascertain. He may have plans for you to stand before a king or president, senator or congressman. Only He can orchestrate that moment in which the destiny of an entire country becomes entwined in the tapestry of your destiny. He was telling Joseph, "Get yourself ready! This is the part in the script where you stand before a king—not to hear a judgment against you, but to actually be received as viable counsel." Wow! Try to imagine yourself in this situation. Feeling sorry for yourself in prison for a non-crime when suddenly the nation's highest ruling power calls you to stand before him because he wants *your* advice.

God's providential timetable inserted Joseph into the highest chambers of the land and requested his interpretation of Pharaoh's unsettling dreams. Joseph remembered the last time he interpreted dreams. They came true, but, for some reason, God delayed his vindication. A couple years later, the surreal setting again changed as God wove yet another texture and color into Joseph's tapestry. Everything about the whole process eliminated human plans and reflected the design of the Master Designer—capable of producing a loving and intricate plan to preserve His people and provide for their inheritance.

When God rescues you He cleans you up, changes your demeanor and puts a smile on that sour face. He says, "Let me clothe you with My Son's robe of righteousness." Joseph had wanted vindication. God didn't allow it. Maybe he wanted his brothers to acknowledge their mistake or his name to be cleared of the charges Potiphar's wife made against him. Maybe not. What God had in mind for now was far greater than personal vindication.

The Highs Always Come After the Lows

While Joseph could never have guessed what was about to happen, God had been busy preparing this tapestry to be showcased just when the times demanded it most. He spent years weaving just the right strands into the life of this 'nobody from nowhere' (Joyce Meyer). While His work in Joseph was not complete, it was far enough along to provide a glimpse into His providential intentions. The king of the greatest nation in the world affirmed and exalted him. And, guess what? Instead of being cleared of the charges and sent home to his family, he was placed second in command to the most powerful man in the world. Let that sink in for a moment. Like Ned Miller crooned in the 1963 country hit song, "From a Jack to a King, from loneliness to a wedding ring . . . .", Joseph went from the lowest low to the highest high. He was given something with which he could be trusted because it had never been the object of his ambition. He wanted his family. Instead, he got Prime Minister of Egypt. The movie, Forest Gump provided many human and humorous insights into the life of someone society had not taken seriously. Throughout the movie, while waiting for a bus, he sat on a park bench with a man recalling different episodes of his life in which he felt ill prepared but yet lived through them anyway. Just as on more than one occasion, he rolled his eyes and told how he met the president and related how he had to go meet him, "*again.*" Joseph was placed in charge of things, "*again.*" When God's providential timetable reveals key players, He usually moves things along quickly. He knows down to the nanosecond when the time is right for His masterpiece to be displayed without diminishing its worth. Joseph went from being a Hebrew slave serving an open-ended prison sentence to Prime Minister in a matter of minutes. He originally ran the household affairs of Potiphar (no pun intended), oversaw the responsibility of the prison while in *that* venue, and now was elevated to the Prime Minister of the country.

There is a place in northern Wyoming between Cody and Burgess Junction called Shell Canyon. Its highway design incorporates a series of switchbacks necessary to traverse the incline of the mountain. I remember pulling over to the side and looking over the edge to the switchbacks below. I counted seven crisscrosses of highway in the seemingly straight-down mountainside. While we were on the incline, all we could see was the rock wall beside us. Yet, when we were on top, we could see the panorama of the beautiful canyon. Many people come to a vantage point in life's journey when they can look back and see a distinct pattern they had not seen before. The events in their lives—especially the painful ones—make sense for the first time. It is like getting to view the tapestry from the underside—then all of a sudden someone turns it around, revealing a beautiful and intricate pattern. Now, God's divine pattern for Joseph's life came into focus rather quickly in light of his sudden and dramatic promotion. Look at 41:41. Pharaoh said to Joseph, *"I hereby put you in charge of the whole land of Egypt."*

It is amazing how quickly things happen on God's providential timetable. Nothing surprises Him and nothing comes back to haunt Him. His plan always seeks the perfection of those who have vowed allegiance to Him and who give Him permission to alter the course of their life to accomplish His will.

There were several areas of prominence that defined the extent of Joseph's newly gained power. He was now responsible for the whole land of Egypt. It was comparable in influence and size only to the Babylonian Empire. Egypt's vast wealth was literally unequalled by any nation on earth. Pharaoh gave Joseph unbridled authority to make any expenditure necessary to accomplish his long-term plan for surviving the coming drought. Joseph wore garments made of fine linen to signify his prestige and power. Additionally, he wore Pharaoh's signet ring and gold chain around his neck. If someone would have told Joseph that morning that he'd have a chain around his neck, he probably would have said, "Been there. Done that." If they said he'd have a "gold chain" he'd have said, "Man, don't *mess* with me." Additionally, Joseph got a company chariot in which to ride as men ran ahead of him clearing the way and making people bow to him. If that was not enough, even Pharaoh told him that he would not issue any decrees unless he first consulted Joseph (41:44).

Take a minute and think of the incredible transformation through which Joseph segued to be in the exact place at the precise time for the strategic purpose for which God had long prepared him. He designed Joseph's tapestry with an ample base from which to illustrate additional weavings as new days demanded fresh insertion of essential textures necessary to reveal the eventual masterpiece. Each new strand inflicted pain from which God formed components of character in the life of this future providential potentate. From dreamer to despised. From father's favored boy to father's future lament. From shepherd's brother to slave block. From hopelessness to hope. From incarceration to interpretation. From anonymity to providential ruler. Joseph came full circle—not too fast, not too slow, but at just the pace to correspond with God's timetable for the ancient world. The dreamer had survived. Now, it was God's time to weave more strands into Joseph's tapestry. However, this time the strands were woven upon the base already woven and began to give the world the impression that the hand of a master designer was at work as new dimensions were about to be added to the already complex tapestry.

A few notable insertions must be placed into this narrative. The Egyptians utilized the names they gave their children to signify the desired direction they intended to provide an indication of what they would become. In some cultures the newborn received the name of the first thing a mother saw after giving birth to the child. If she looked up and saw a bird in flight, the name might represent something free and given to fantasy. The downside of that tradition is almost humorous. If a woman saw a dog scratching fleas, the child's name might represent something else. Needless to say, an individual's name often became a precursor to how they were perceived throughout life.

Pharaoh decided to engineer perceptions and opted to change Joseph's name to Zaphenath-Paneah. The word *Nath* meant, "God speaks and lives." If Joseph was to carry weight as a ruler in Egypt, his name had to represent power and authority. Pharaoh wanted people to regard Joseph as deity and not an ordinary man. He wanted to remove all semblances to simply being a spokesman for the king and replace it with a name that automatically generated fear and respect among the people. Additionally, Pharaoh arranged the marriage of Joseph to Asenath. This couple, by their names alone, represented deity. Their names provided the necessary credentials for the people to view this couple as more than just another royal couple. Their names became the link to the most prestigious religious position in the kingdom.

Are you beginning to understand what can happen when the time of God's providential fulfillment has come? Do you understand more clearly the difference between chastisement and punishment? *"My son, do not despise the chastening of the Lord, nor be discouraged when you are rebuked by Him; for whom the Lord loves He chastens, and scourges every son whom He receives."* (Heb. 12:5-6) God had a plan for Joseph when nobody else gave him a second thought. His plan included his birth order, his father's insistence that the boy remain around home while his brothers did all the work, and his favored status with his father. Everything he did through his early years became a strand in his tapestry. There could be no missing strands. It had to be complete. The resentment by his brothers facilitated his being sold as a potential slave and eventually ending up in his present position as the Prime Minister Egyptians associated with deity. Only God can put something like that together.

Humankind is too narrow-minded and myopic. God sees the big picture and knows when He has to chastise a main character in life's scenario. He knows when to exalt and when to abase. He alone knows the balance of what is too much adulation and what is too much chastisement. You must believe that God has a plan for your life and that most of what has happened to you to this point has been to refine and correct your missteps. God *always* produces a masterpiece. He alone can turn the whiners into winners. He taught Joseph some painful but powerful lessons. At this point in the narrative, Joseph was 30 years old. The last 13 years of his life finally began making sense.

Charles Spurgeon, in his book, *God's Providence*, provided timeless insight into how the individual views the difficulties associated with their life. He points out, "Providence is wonderfully intricate. Ah! You want always to see through Providence, do you not? You never will, I assure you. You have not eyes good enough. You want to see what good that affliction was to you; you must believe it. You want to see how it can bring good to the soul; you may be enabled in a little time; but you cannot see it now;

you must believe it. Honor God by trusting Him" (p. 19). If God allowed humankind to view the inner workings of His providential plan, the chance of their interfering with the plan becomes a probability. God knows human nature. He created it. He knows that our propensity for curiosity and eventual control requires necessary safeguards to keep the plan on track.

Richard Sibbes once stated, "The winter prepares the earth for the spring, so do afflictions sanctified prepare the soul for glory." Joseph dared to hold a ray of hope in his heart—otherwise, he could not have endured the agenda forced upon his life. He endured many winters that seemingly lasted longer than their normal cycles. He lived in hardship and great difficulty, yet, required only a shave and change of clothing to become presentable in the king's court. When God's providential timetable requires action, things move quickly, purposefully, and result in both the display and function of a masterpiece.

Joseph not only survived the pressure from the hand of the Master Weaver, but used it for the glory and honor of God. Thirteen years marked his life with the pain and rejection few could bear—yet; he would not and could not forget how God worked in his life during that time. The Lord had prepared him well. A. W. Tozer wrote, "It is doubtful whether God can bless a man greatly until He has hurt him deeply." I am old enough to remember the punishment for disobedience and self-will. However, I appreciate knowing that punishment and chastisement is not the same thing. Chastisement may hurt as much or more than punishment, but its purpose is to realign the course of a person's life and insure arrival at a pre-determined point. Yes, that may hurt, but it will not produce the level of fear that punishment produces. Punishment produces an elicited response. "If you do that again, I will punish you more severely!" Chastisement produces productive understanding of the things necessary to become a better person. When God chooses to chastise us, we become more usable in His plan. We gain an understanding of His great love and the lengths He is willing to go to produce a thing of beauty and an instrument of righteousness.

Every high-level leadership position holds a price tag. Fortunately, Joseph's preparation was also spiritual. With every difficulty, his relationship with God grew. I fully believe that God gives us all certain choices at various points along our journey in life. We either persevere and grow, or we turn away and take another path—a detour from His plan. If we choose to allow God to order our steps and stops, we must pay the price or pay the penalty. A masterpiece's value stems from two things: the amount of clear detail and the amount of artistic intention. Both produce pain in the process but magnificent beauty in the product.

If you think about it for a moment, you would have to agree that Joseph's elevation was one thing, but the responsibility of his position could have been overwhelming. Fortunately, God wove strands into his tapestry that both prepared him for his day and produced strategic leadership capable of insuring the survival of an entire race of people.

Look at Genesis 41:47-57. This passage relates how he stored up huge quantities of grain—like the sand of the sea—in every city. The surplus was so great that Joseph even stopped keeping records. Think of the challenge to guarantee honesty and integrity in this huge operation. And, if maintaining honesty and integrity the first seven years was a problem, just think of the second seven years when people were faced with survival. Chapter 41:56-57 reveals that the famine spread throughout their world. Joseph had to administer the distribution of food not only to the Egyptians, but to all who traveled to Egypt to buy food as well. At the tender age of 30, he could never have handled this world-class task without an intensive and experience-oriented course in management. He was amazed at what happened when God's providential timetable authenticated the personal process through which he had finally emerged.

Doing Life in Real Time:

Have you been impatient with God's timing? Is there a situation you think you must manipulate? We are predictable, aren't we? Maybe God's providential plan has yet to be fully revealed. That simply means more time in the process before the product is ready.

Two applications:

1. If you do not know the Lord and have never trusted Jesus Christ to forgive your sins, you do not need to wait any longer. It is always God's time for someone to accept His Son. 2 Corinthians 6:2 says, *"In an acceptable time I have heard you, and in the day of salvation I have helped you. Behold, now is the accepted time; behold, now is the day of salvation."* Don't put off that decision. Wouldn't you like to know the account is settled? He wants to forgive you. He wants to give you hope. He wants you to understand that His chastisement does not indicate

disfavor. He is bringing you to a strategic moment in your life when all that matters to you will be to love and please Him and to accept His wonderful plan for the rest of your life.

2. If you *do* know the Lord but you realize you have not trusted His plan for your life or current circumstances, you need to allow Him the proper place in your life. It doesn't please Him when you worry needlessly over things you really can't control. Is your life in His hands, or not?

Here's Your Handle:

Be patient. Persevere. You'll be amazed at what doors are opened to you when God's providential timetable allows you to see the other side of your tapestry.

Jim Beaird

Chapter 6

Getting Past the Past

Whenever God guides a person through a time of rejection and pain, He always has a plan for the individual's restoration and health.

What is the greatest pain a person can experience? Is it the pain of failure? Is it the pain of financial loss? How about the pain of a relationship gone sour or the discomfort associated with a physical ailment? Arguably, the most debilitating pain a person can feel is the pain of rejection. Psychologists maintain that rejection from those you love can cause an emotional pain that sends shock waves through your self-esteem. The after-effects of rejection leave cracks in an individual's underpinning and everything he or she tries to build upon the fissured foundation eventually falls apart from insufficient cohesion. Struggles to make sense out of everyday events become all consuming and exhausting. A sense of worthlessness dominates their thinking as they try to apply a familiar metric to the malaise of real-time living—only to realize that nothing from their past fits into what's actually happening in the present. When a person looses his or her sense of self worth through a series of rejections, the danger of self-inflicted death is at its greatest point. Without a familiar template in which to process recurring and chronic rejection, an individual simply gives up and rationalizes that a second or two of pain is better than a lifetime without acceptance or love.

If you stop and think about it, Joseph was a prime candidate for all these feelings and more. His experiences were far more intense than any of us will probably ever have to endure. He came to understand a great many feelings not usually associated with the normal course of life. So much happened in such a short period of time. He came to understand false accusations and punishment for something he did not do. He even helped a fellow prisoner to understand what was ahead, only to be left behind in the prison without any hope of vindication. Yet, he was just as human as anyone reading this book. God had a way of orchestrating several events and factors that produced beautiful and harmonious music into his heart—once filled with a cacophony of harsh and dissonant sounds.

As our modern vernacular would put it, "Ok!

Now *that's* what I'm talking about." For the first time in thirteen years, Joseph could actually take a long, refreshing breath. To be certain, he probably thought this moment would never come, but here he was, reeling from the pace of events that would alter his life forever. His tapestry was taking shape nicely! His life would forever be linked with the providence of God in conversations of future millenniums. God did not take a shortcut to produce a demonstration of His capabilities. He did not use an old design. His thoughts were both on the process at hand in developing a malleable instrument and procuring a life-saving posterity for every single remnant of humankind.

I read about a man who had served many years in prison on a life sentence without the possibility of parole accused of a crime he denied committing. Suddenly, he gained freedom and exoneration from the crime when a man came forward and admitted to the crime—even giving details that only the guilty could know. He gained his release twenty-five years after his initial incarceration. While in jail, he lost everything—his family, his home, his reputation. But something about this particular story intrigued me. The man was not bitter. Rather, his newfound freedom refused to allow him to dwell on the injustice that robbed him of everything he once had.

He savored his new lot in life and anticipated traveling his new road. The court system expunged his record so he would never have to reveal his "former convict" status when applying for a job. Upon hearing the man's story via newscasts and radio, many businesses stepped forward to help right the wrong by providing him not only with a place to live but a myriad of opportunities in which to start his new life.

I can't help but think of Joseph and wonder what he must have felt. Remember Potiphar's wife—the woman on the prowl that tried unsuccessfully to seduce him on repeated occasions? Her servants must have known what really happened, but they were smart enough to know who buttered their bread.

When word broke that Joseph was put in charge of all Egypt, these same servants—who could have spoken in his defense, wondered if he would exact revenge and settle the score. Perish the thought. Joseph had more important things to do than to execute petty revenge on people who shared his former social status. Now, Joseph was even Potiphar's boss. Joseph was beginning to understand just what could happen in God's providential timetable. No need to fabricate an imagination of what might have happened to the servants who knew the truth about the lecherous woman responsible for the last several years of Joseph's life. Time to move on. Don't get stuck in the past. God still has a plan.

We need to note something at this particular time in the story of God's providence in the life of Joseph. He was free from prison and he was free in his spirit. His sudden promotion from prisoner to prime minister had to make things much more tolerable. He went from being looked down upon to someone to whom everyone had to give an account. He actually received the same respect and honor as Pharaoh himself. While he was the subject of God's handiwork, he was still subject to Pharaoh. He had to juggle competing thoughts that tempted him to show off his new power—kind of enjoy it for a while, and yet realize that God had orchestrated this veneration and vindication for a purpose. Joseph might easily have succumbed to the temptation to wield his power "just because he could." The scriptural narrative does not imply that Joseph ever succumbed to prideful behavior. He was probably tempted as he'd ride his chariot through the streets of towns and see people bowing down to him, but he knew in his heart that he was where God had placed him and could just as easily be removed. He would not risk so much for so little—especially now that he knew, apart from God's plan—he was nothing.

We are frequently tempted to take credit for what the Lord allows—as if by virtue of our own abilities we are where we are—or we have what we have. The 45th verse relates Joseph's marriage to Asenath, the daughter of a pagan priest. She came to understand quickly that Joseph's God was the one true God. This marriage was the first time since he was separated from his father that he has been able to enjoy a close relationship with anybody. He came to love someone who would return his love. Joseph must have spent hours relating to Asenath some of the hurts of his past. Her friendship and love helped Joseph through the time of transition from his interesting past to his vital role in Egypt and Israel's history. Her marriage to Joseph provided the accruements of the socially elite while also providing her with an exceptional man. While Pharaoh had arranged the marriage, it was pre-ordained by God. The providential plan included a suitable "reimbursement" for all the loneliness Joseph endured while God prepared him for the years to come.

There are a few observations you might find

interesting. Even though Asenath was the daughter of a pagan priest, Joseph did not allow himself to be swayed by her pagan background. The Egyptian society and government was one in which men in high political positions had many wives and women in their harem as a demonstration of their power. But, Asenath was the only woman in Joseph's life. She was the only wife he ever had. He didn't even follow his father's example, but retained a monogamous relationship with her. In that day, in that setting and with all that power, what an incredible testimony to the commitment of marriage. While Joseph could have had entire harems at his beck and call, he chose to lovingly embrace the woman God held back just for him. His refusal to take other wives testifies to his being content with whom God had provided to share his life. His tapestry took on an added dimension of meaning and purpose with his new life partner.

Genesis 41:50 relates that before the years of famine, Asenath gave birth to two sons. The names Joseph gave his sons are a significant clue in understanding how God brought restoration to him. Centuries later, Solomon would write, *"Sons are a heritage from the Lord, children a reward from him."* **Ps. 127:3** Joseph named his first son MANASSEH – literally meaning, "one who causes to forget." He gave the explanation as to why he chose that particular name. *"It is because God has made me forget all my trouble and all my father's household"* (v. 51). Whenever God guides a person through a time of rejection and pain, He always has a plan for the individual's restoration and health. Joseph still had both sets of memories—the fond and the not so fond. His humanity retained questions about why his own brothers had betrayed him and why he had been imprisoned for having integrity and why vindication had taken so long. However, Joseph recognized that God's tapestry weaving on his behalf had produced an incredible panorama of potential for which no human could take credit.

Questions naturally flood to the surface given the meaning of Manasseh. Did he forget the humiliating and painful rejection by his brothers? Did he ever forget the putrid smell in the pit as he awaited an unknown fate? Did he forget the long journey on foot in the arid heat as his captors relished their potential profit? Did he forget the humiliation of being stripped bare and displayed like merchandise in the slave market? Did he forget the long hours in which he thought about his father and little brother Benjamin?

He doubtless spent many sleepless nights trying

to sort out just why his life took a left turn at the right turn signal and why nobody came looking for him. His apparent abandonment fueled his oft-repeated question-answer sessions with himself—never arriving at a plausible explanation as to how something like this could happen to a father's favorite son. The details of these events were etched indelibly in his mind. He could never forget them. What, then, did God allow Joseph to forget through the birth of his first son, Manasseh?

Pain. Forget the pain. Don't hold onto it like a badge of honor. Do you have the propensity to idolize pain for its attention-gaining attributes? Let go of it and it will let go of you. Emotional pain can be almost addictive for people who feel they do not have anything else with which to parlay into sympathy. Truthfully, they must be willing to let go and move on. God will heal the hurt caused by those events in your life, too, but you have to be willing to get on with life. You'll still have the memories but not the pain. Most of us can point to a scar somewhere on our body. We remember the event that caused the scar, but we can't remember the pain unless we really try—then we only remember the *fact* of our suffering and not the actual pain itself. We all have some emotional scars. Scars are OK. Scars are a sign of healing—a point of closure. If you remove the scars, you remove the memory of what God brought you through.

I remember holding my first son under my arm like a football. I was so proud to be his dad. I fully intended to be the best dad in the whole world. Yet, my wife came close to death—literally—to give birth to him. Through a rare condition that occurs in a very small percentage of deliveries, she had complications after he made his grand entrance. I was the first father/husband to ever be allowed in the delivery room in Sheridan County, Wyoming. After my son was born, the doctors sensed something was wrong and asked me to leave the room. I felt helpless. I moved a chair from the waiting room to the hallway just outside the delivery room. I waited. Soon, nurses began running past me with bags of blood and IV lines. Having no medical training and no idea of what was happening on the other side of the door, I began to imagine the worst. Nobody provided details—just frantic activity indicating they were dealing with a life-threatening situation. After a while, they emerged from the delivery room and wheeled my young wife past me en route to the recovery room. Pale as the sheets in which she was wrapped, her eyes were shut. Watching her disappear down the hall, a nurse saw my obvious concern and stepped to my side. "We think she will be ok. Time will tell, but right now, she needs to rest until she regains consciousness. Please leave us your phone number and we will call you when she stabilizes."

As I drove home through the spring sleet, I spoke out loud as if God was a passenger in my car. My words bordered on cynical as I tried in vain to get a response from a God who, apparently, did not care. My arguments focused on what I had given up to enter the ministry and how God should treat his children better. We sacrificed to serve our small parish and, for three years, did not receive a salary in any form from the church. Did my faith experience an ebb tide during that difficult trial? Yes. While my youthful enthusiasm and reckless faith had sustained me up to that point, for the first time in my life, I felt at a loss for what to say and what to believe God could do in this crisis. God and I argued for a while as I paced the floor in our basement apartment. Having relieved my pained spirit of the sinful vitriol, I noticed that I had not been struck dead. God had been listening to me and allowing me to vent—as humans often do. Then something changed. I remember standing in front of the fireplace as I told God that I'd serve him no matter what happened. No matter what. The phone rang. It was the hospital telling me that she had stabilized and I could come and see her. That phone call provided both a reality check to bring me back into the physical world and an assurance that:

God has a plan. He knows what's ahead.
He's shaping a world-changer.

Now, when we look at our *three* sons, we remember the event that took place forty plus years ago in northern Wyoming. Somehow, though, we do not feel the pain and fear we felt then. Like Joseph, we are caused to forget past pain because of present blessing. For Joseph, just holding that little boy in his arms must have brought incredible emotional healing. God is faithful. Always has been. Always will be. He alone provides healing for emotional pain that threatens to cripple our perspective of the work of art He's weaving into our personal tapestries.

Asenath gave Joseph a second son. Again, he chose a name that focused upon what God was doing in his life at that particular time. He named his second son, EPHRAIM—literally, *"God has made me fruitful"* (v. 52). God indeed made Joseph fruitful! He blessed him with a beautiful family of his own, gave him wealth and power second only to Pharaoh, and success in preparing for the preservation of millions of people. Joseph had not forgotten the pain of the past, but in naming his second son Ephraim, he gave the clear signal that he was ready to move on with his life. His suffering had left a scar; yet, there was no pain as he rejoiced in the blessings of God. He had healed. He understood *both* trial and triumph.

When you heal, you can face the thing from which you have been running. When you heal, you can know your tapestry has highs and lows—things necessary to provide aesthetic texture and captivating design. When you heal, you can feel the sun again and know God has brought you out from under your trial.

Doing Life in Real Time:

Have you resented God's intervention in your life? Do you feel you have forsaken opportunities that could have provided a more substantial life and income for you and your family?

Do you feel that God left you somewhere in the past and you never caught up with everyone else?

1. Be willing to relive the memories of the events that caused so much pain.

2. Confess to God that you have not moved past the event(s) and desire to experience His healing of the past and blessings of the present.

3. Embrace TODAY and TOMORROW and leave yesterday behind.

Here's Your Handle:

Quit navigating your life using only a rear-view mirror. Get past the past. Embrace what God provides for you in your present and future.

Chapter 7

The Family Secret

Humankind continually deals with the damage from too much exposure to harmful elements in relationships.

The previous chapter in this commentary on Joseph and God's divine providence dealt with the healing of life's greatest pain—*rejection*. Few things can compete with the pain a person feels when rejected by those he or she loves. A series of rejections magnifies the pain greatly. Recovery from the effects of rejection—especially if it has been perceived as true and accurate, requires both the benefit of time and immersion in a healing atmosphere. As I pointed out in the preceding chapter, the pain of rejection is often so great that it mutes out well-intentioned advice from others who do not know the pain being suffered nor do they rightly discern remedial steps to recovery. Everyone has advice to give. Not all advice provides assurance the pain will someday end and become only a distant memory. God blessed Joseph and helped him experience healing from that emotional pain by giving him two sons, Manasseh and Ephraim whose names meant, "The Lord has caused me to forget," and "The Lord has blessed me in the land of my affliction."

The Second Step

There is distinctly a second step in the process of going through the healing of life's greatest pain. Countless sermons, lessons, books, and video series abound on the subject. However, I trust your attention to this narrative compels you to complete step two and, as I said in the last chapter, 'get on with life.' Empty and emotionless lives testify to the failure of countless individuals to escape the clutches of unforgiveness. That is why the next step becomes an ultimate test of your willingness to receive God's healing. In a word, the second step is "forgiveness." Don't close the book—not just yet. You recall having heard the need to forgive but its message has yet to impact your whole rationale regarding relationships gone badly. Someone shattered your life into millions of useless shards and you are left alone to pick up the pieces and try to regain a semblance of normalcy. So, do we ever really master this forgiveness thing? Can we ever say, "I am finished with this and will not be captive to its accusations and implications any longer," or does our memory of the pain draw us back to the talons that once pierced our hearts? Do we ever really escape? First of all, let me say that it is not a matter of escaping something that has power over you. It is rather a matter of our reconciling the price (which we could not afford) has been paid and our freedom awaits our decision to believe what God said. I have taught dozens of times on forgiveness and each time the Lord reminds me to release something that seems to be stunting my spiritual growth. He reminds me that practicing what I preach is not a matter of doing what *I* said to do, but doing what *He* said to do.

Jesus taught that we must love our enemies and pray for those who despitefully use or persecute us. Even as He hung upon the cross, He asked His Father to forgive those who had nailed Him there and said they didn't realize what they were doing. We find it difficult to gain such perspective amidst the pain of our trial. Think of that coworker who took your idea and got promoted. To cover their tracks, they lied to the boss about you and put you in the unemployment ranks. While that may be an extreme example of an initial cause for unforgiveness, it illustrates the point. Or, perhaps a family member took credit for something you did and received adulation and praise from your parents. Maybe that sibling orchestrated a well-planned scheme to take credit for most of what you did well and you never got credit for any of it. Whatever caused the formation of a bitter and unforgiving spirit in you— either in an instance that simply occurred unexpectedly, or in an ongoing fabrication of someone's accomplishments at your expense, it will only hurt you—until you recognize its potential for isolating you from an otherwise fruitful relationship.

The Price of Retaliation

The temptation to retaliate testifies to humankind's propensity for self-preservation. A store employee treated a wealthy man rudely. The man promptly went to its owner and bought the business and fired the employee because, he said, "It's the principle of the thing that matters." It was his way of retaliating, even though it cost him a great deal. Retaliation finds its root in the human need to be right—to win at any cost. Needless to say, the former employee probably only learned that if a person has enough money or power, they can usually get their way. Their form of retaliation would be to never buy anything from that store again—just to show them!

I mention the wealthy man and the store employee for a reason. The same interchange takes place in marriages, homes, places of employment, and even churches. Someone goes to great length to prove a point. Someone else takes it wrong and decides to boycott the relationship—you know, the *cold* treatment. Someone gets offended and decides to make their *own* point. Before long, nobody can accurately describe how the fracture took place or why.

Trigger Points

A painful type of short-term injury is a rug burn. When my sons were young, we used to wrestle on the living room carpet. I often collected a series of "strawberries" where the top layer or two of skin got removed from rubbing against the carpet and then exposed nerves that seem to short circuit in the fresh air or against a shirt sleeve or pant leg. You have probably been there, done that, right? Then, usually the lady of the house says, "I told you not to wrestle in the house. It's your own fault if you get rug burns!" We raised three champion sons and, to this day, I still insist that it was the rug burns that made them tough—at least that's my story and I'm sticking to it.

We can forget *some* things and "get on" with life. But there are also times when we come face-to-face with the one who hurt us, and the recurring pain becomes an emotional "strawberry" that once again short circuits and reminds us of both the event and the pain associated with it. After we moved to Florida we experienced the same physical feeling with sunburn. I recall a particular time when I spent too much time walking the beaches without sunscreen protection. That night, I could not sleep on my back. The next day I went shirtless to the back yard and the sunshine immediately reminded me of my fool-hearted romp on the beach the day before. It only took a few seconds to reignite the fire in my skin that had me scrambling for shade. Whether it is rug burn or sunburn, the damage takes a while to repair and the feelings associated with the resultant pain come easily. Those are points that trigger reminders of the painful encounter with what caused the "strawberries."

Humankind continually deals with the damage from too much exposure to harmful elements in relationships. The human psyche is fragile and easily resets to the default of survival—particularly when faced with how one's emotional pain originated. Simply seeing a person in public who hurt you becomes a mental and emotional struggle to maintain order in your fragile balance between living each new day as it comes and being forced to relive the painful event that inflicted in you an emotional rug burn or sunburn. You thought you were through the phase of dealing with the virulent pain that nearly torpedoed your life and now it happens all over again—in your mind and heart. You are not free from it. You see that now and begin to wonder whether or not you will *ever* be. Human skin repairs itself quickly, but the human emotional system requires divine intervention to once again become a healthy reflection of God's grace in a person's life.

The offense some people feel as a result of a fractured relationship literally becomes a badge of honor to them. They wear it proudly and decide not to let go of the offense because it became a way to punish their offender. They withhold forgiveness and justify its continued residence in their heart. A victim mentality drives their relational response to the offender's actions—whether recent or not, and keeps them in a prison of their own making. The keys hang within their reach, but they remain in the dark recesses of the prison because it now represents safety to them. No interaction with the offender, no chance for additional pain, and no need to traverse the minefield of feelings associated with whatever started the whole destructive cycle.

We already caught a glimpse of Joseph's true character and saw the unusual healing that God brought to his heart. Now, we're about to witness how he handles forgiveness. Whether this incident sets a precedent in the "forgiveness hall of fame" or not, it accurately represents feelings and emotions everyone experiences at one time or another. Some people *look for* chances to take up an offense and fall easy victims to the trespass traps. Others willfully determine to see the best in everyone—often to the extreme of naivety. Joseph did not look for a chance to be offended nor was he naïve. The providence of God wove into his life the textured strands of pain and hardship necessary to provide him with wisdom capable of preserving the life of a nation and a race of people. He had not manipulated situations so he could gain sympathy nor had he walked blindly into the recent phase of his life involving his imprisonment and eventual elevation to administration and oversight of the king's resources.

When Jacob saw that there was grain in Egypt, Jacob said to his sons, "Why do you look at one another?" 2 And he said, indeed I have heard that there is grain in Egypt; go down to that place and buy for us there, that we may live and not die." 3 So Joseph's ten brothers went down to buy grain in Egypt. (42:1-3)

The years of abundance ceased and the famine made its impact felt in Egypt and the surrounding countries. Without the advantage of the evening news or Internet, Jacob heard that grain had been stored in Egypt and could be bought. He told his sons to get off their backsides and go to Egypt to buy grain. The famine continued oppressing the land and its inhabitants. They faced the danger of dying from hunger. The first hapless victims would be the animals and then, a short time later, hunger and disease would take the rest of them. They faced odds over which none of them had control. Their own crops fell victim to the drought and even what they had stored up offered meager chances for survival. Something needed to happen outside of their normal course of life so, being the patriarch and usually having the final say over his descendants, Jacob decided to send his sons to Egypt to buy grain. However, according to verse 4, Jacob feared his youngest son, Benjamin, might be harmed so he kept him at home while his ten brothers traveled to Egypt for grain. It had been over twenty years since Jacob's beloved Joseph had been killed. His body had never been found and he had not even had the opportunity to grieve over the body. Joseph had become a missing person with no other explanation then that a wild animal had ripped him up and drug him away into the wilderness. He did not want something to happen to his youngest son like what had happened to Joseph.

Unbroken Patterns

Do you see a pattern there? *Someone* had not let go of the past or its tragic intersection with the life of his family. Jacob really did not forgive his older sons for their failure to protect his beloved youngest son from the wiles of the wilderness. He blamed them for his loss and they all knew it. I suspect that over the years, Jacob dropped conversational "hints" as to their inability to protect or rescue Joseph from the calamity purported in the brothers' vindictive narrative. Perhaps a bit of mistrust flavored his perception of the remaining older sons. Additionally, he did not really trust them to take care of Benjamin, his youngest. They lived with a father who had not regarded them as worthy of his blessing or praise and had simply carried out the expectations of their family system of governance. One might suspect that they all knew they walked on thin ice and did not want to exacerbate their father's lamented loss. Past failure held them all captive in the prison of deceit and its consequent uncertainty.

We have taken several chapters to get to this

point in understanding God's unique way of dealing with those He prepares for life's greatest tasks.

Remember,

God has a plan. He knows what's ahead.
He's shaping a world-changer.

It is necessary to keep that in mind because it applies to our lives in today's world amidst all its uncertainties and all its failed promises. Once the child of God loses sight of the Master's hand at the tapestry loom of his or her life, all perspective and hope fades like a dimming light in a dark tunnel. Once godly perspective loses relevance in a life, decisions take on a self-sufficiency that only leads to poor decision-making and produces a tainted version of what God had originally intended. The providential intersection of His hand upon historical events demands the participation of key players in key situations. Some unwittingly drive the situation to a point of crisis to produce a sense of need and emergency. Nothing drives participation like desperation! Others fit the category of influential individuals capable of seeing the big picture and are able to re-evaluate everything relating to the once comfortable world in which they all lived.

Things seemed to be going smoothly for Joseph. He had been correct in predicting the famine. Nobody questioned his decisions—yet, power had not corrupted him. He dealt fairly with all who came to buy grain. He validated God's choice of him as the one to oversee the event designed to reshape the future of the entire mid-east region of the world. Joseph proved by his integrity that the provincial world was in good hands and that God was true to His plan.

Remember what I said about strawberries? We're about to see if Joseph has any. Another divine intersection is about to take place at a time Joseph least expected. The stage had been set for God's plan to resolve the pain of his past and provide opportunity for God's providential plan to emerge.

> *5 And the sons of Israel went to buy grain among those who journeyed, for the famine was in the land of Canaan. 6 Now Joseph was governor over the land; and it was he who sold to all the people of the land. And Joseph's brothers came and bowed down before him with their faces to the earth. 7 Joseph saw his brothers and recognized them, but he acted as a stranger to them and spoke roughly to them. Then he said to them, "Where do you come from?" And they said, "From the land of Canaan to buy food." 8 So*

Joseph recognized his brothers, but they did not recognize him" (42:5-8).

When his brothers arrived in Egypt, they were ushered into his presence. They had no idea that he was the governor of all Egypt. Their last sight was of him lying on the bottom of the pit—probably crying—and then he was simply carried off to a foreign land and never heard from again. Their problem had been solved, the lie perpetuated, and their lives changed forever. As Joseph looked up at those standing in line to buy grain, he recognized his brothers. His eyes must have focused like lasers on the foreigners as they waited their turn to buy grain. Twenty-two years had passed since he last saw their faces, but he recognized them. Their beards set them apart from the clean-shaven Egyptian men. His emotional strawberries started to flair with exposure to the memory of what had transpired those many years ago and the many trials in which he had to remain faithful to his God.

Providential "Strawberries"

Joseph was nearly forty-four by this time. Everything about his appearance reflected the Egyptian culture as he stood before them. You can understand why they didn't recognize him. From their perspective, he was the last person they expected to ever see again. He was a teenager when they last saw him. They had no clue as to what happened to him after the Mideanite traders took him away. They certainly did not expect to find him elevated to *second man* in Egypt! Now Joseph began to sense some short-circuiting. His strawberries were flashing their warning. I can only imagine that as he stood before them, he tried in vain to suppress the emotions that threatened to twist his gut into knots. He looked at them . . . Reuben, the oldest brother who had actually been responsible for saving his life; Leah's sons, Simeon, Levi, Judah, Issachar, and Zebulun. There was Dan and Naphtali the sons of Bilhah; and Dan and Asher, sons of Zilpah. But wait . . . . Something was not right as he scanned the area for clues. Someone was missing. *Where* was his youngest brother, Benjamin?

Can you imagine what questions must have flooded his mind? Is Jacob still alive? Where is Benjamin—is he still alive? What are the attitudes of my brothers now? What is their relationship with God? Remember his dreams in which he shared that the sheaves of grain and the sun, moon, and eleven stars would all bow down to him? Now he looks at them as they are commanded to bow before him. They were *bowing* before him! He was in a position of honor, power and authority over them twenty-two years after his dreams of them.

Then, a plan began to crystalize in his mind. He thought through several options including placing them in prison—just to let them know how it felt. After a few moments of spontaneous thought, he decided to accuse them of being spies. He still needed answers from them and placing them under arrest—even for a short time, could accomplish everything he wanted to accomplish. Or, perhaps, he just wanted to make sure they did not evade his inquisition.

As their brother, he knew their nature. He knew their capability for deceit and self-preservation. Night after lonely night in the Egyptian jail must have provided him with ample opportunity to rehearse the improbable future meeting with his brothers—what he would say, how he would act, questions he would ask. Joseph *had* to know about his father and younger brother. As his accusation of being spies sent fear into their hearts, they began to spill the beans and give Joseph all the information he needed.

"Then Joseph remembered the dreams which he had dreamed about them, and said to them, "You are spies! You have come to see the nakedness of the

land!" 10 And they said to him, "No, my lord, but your servants have come to buy food. 11 We are all one man's sons; we are honest men; your servants are not spies." 12 But he said to them, "No, but you have come to see the nakedness of the land." 13 And they said, "Your servants are twelve brothers, the sons of one man in the land of Canaan; and in fact, the youngest is with our father today, and one is no more." 14 But Joseph said to them, "It is as I spoke to you, saying, 'You are spies!' 15 In this manner you shall be tested: By the life of Pharaoh, you shall not leave this place unless your youngest brother comes here. 16 Send one of you, and let him bring your brother; and you shall be kept in prison, that your words may be tested to see whether there is any truth in you; or else, by the life of Pharaoh, surely you are spies!" 17 So he put them all together in prison three days" (42:9-17).

His conditions were severe. The youngest brother must join them. One of them would return home and get Benjamin while the other nine stayed in jail. Joseph had to be tough with them in order to get at the truth and understand the state of his father's health. It is here that I must add that I don't think Joseph really had a viable plan in motion. He really didn't know exactly what to do so he had them put in jail three days while he thought this thing through. The only thing of which we can be certain is that he never really intended to do them harm. It simply was not in his nature to be vengeful and punitive toward his only brothers—even though they felt it was all right to sell him away from the comfort of his family then cover it with a lie to their father. The three days could have a compounding effect on them and, as he watched them squirm, he would learn more about how they felt, why they did to him what they did, and the actual state of his father's health. His end game was nobler than their treacherous act that sent him to this region for such a time as this.

Verse 13 records that his brothers gave him some of the needed information. Jacob and Benjamin were alive. So *that* much was settled. A plan began to formulate and Joseph pursued the chances of reuniting his family, settling the score with his brothers, and seeing his loving father and same-age sibling brother. He knew that if he did not use his influence and authority to press the issue of this providential meeting, he would never again see his father or younger brother. Prior to this date in time, his brothers had only viewed him as "the Dreamer" and not a valued member of the family. His position of endearment to his father didn't help his cause either. But, he had the upper hand. He was in the driver seat and capable of taking this event anywhere he chose. He set the price. *"You will not leave this place unless your youngest brother comes here"* (15).

Joseph wisely put his brothers in prison for three days. As he thought things through, he apparently concluded that his original decision to keep all the brothers and send one home to retrieve Benjamin was not a good plan. Seeing only one son return might be too hard on his father. Besides, one brother could not carry enough grain to feed his family and in-laws. The logistics could not support such an arrangement. However, with his brothers in prison for three days, Joseph had time to iron out the details and officially launch the plan to reunite his family.

"Then Joseph said to them the third day, "Do this and live, for I fear God" (18).

The hard hearts of Joseph's brothers began to soften as their guilt pushed its way to the surface. For more than twenty years they had lived with the memory of what they did, yet could not speak of it to anyone—not even their own wives. They could not risk word getting back to Jacob. Their silence did not negate the compounding effect of the guilt. I believe they even began to distrust each other as their once jovial times around the evening fire took on an ominous tone and they simply tolerated each other's presence because they did not know how to process their great iniquity.

> *"Then they said to one another, "We are truly guilty concerning our brother, for we saw the anguish of his soul when he pleaded with us, and we would not hear; therefore, this distress has come upon us. And Reuben answered then, saying, 'Did I not speak to you saying, 'Do not sin against the boy'; and you would not listen? Therefore behold, his blood is now required of us"*(42:21-22).

With every hour that went by inside the prison walls, Joseph's brothers began giving language to the very thing they had decided to never speak about again. Joseph understood every word they said and realized his decision to incarcerate them aided his overall plan. Not knowing that he could understand them, they talked freely about the pain they all felt and how its payback finally caught up with them. As he listened to them, he learned that they were remorseful for what they did to their "long-lost-brother," and acknowledged the responsibility for his blood. Joseph must have felt his own throat tighten as he witnessed God's conviction and redemptive process in real time as they continued to vent their conviction as to why they found themselves in a foreign prison accused of being spies. Yet, Joseph realized that God was at work in them just as He had been at work in his life. It was now time for them to confront their demons once and for all and gain opportunity to make things right. Joseph just let them keep talking. He saw the healing begin to come as they verbalized the pain they previously could only suppress. Perhaps some of them wept openly as they stripped the insulation from the hotwires connecting their consciences. While they feared the eventual outcome of their time in prison, they welcomed the healing that came with their confessions of the heinous lie they had perpetrated upon their father. An acceptance of their deserved fate began to come into focus. As Joseph listened from a distance, he realized the confessions were accurate and heartfelt. Water under the bridge. Nothing they could do now except accept their fate and face the music.

Narratives abound in which an individual suppresses the truth about something that ended up marring someone's life—perhaps even to the point of death. They live with the memories and fight daily to suppress the truth because to do so would be to put their own family in jeopardy. The pain only compounds itself and never goes away. Maybe they told a lie that ended up getting someone with whom they worked fired. With the unemployment came family stress, eventual bankruptcy then divorce. A family was torn apart from the lie that started it all— seemingly innocent at first but had a compounding effect that literally ruined a family. If only the individual who lied could go back and un-tell the lie, but the truth is that once an event takes place, it is permanent—indelibly etched in the record of personal integrity. Perhaps heaven keeps a record of everyone whose life was ruined by someone else's lies. Maybe God even uses those lies to redirect an individual's life so they can be used mightily of Him. If so, He gives healing and forgiveness to both the perpetrator's repentant heart and to the victim whose life has been forever altered.

> *"And he turned himself away from them and wept. Then he returned to them again, and talked with them. And he took Simeon from them and bound him before their eyes"* (24).

The Opus Before the Aria

Joseph had to get alone. He could no longer keep himself composed in their presence. As he began to weep, all the emotional pain he'd felt over the years blended with feelings of relief and even joy. Yet, it was still not the time to reveal his identity to them. They were sorry—but he had yet to ascertain whether they were sorry for what they did or sorry that it was now catching up with them. Joseph stuck with his original plan. He kept Simeon and had him bound before their eyes and sent the others back to Canaan with enough grain to feed their families. Politically speaking, he needed to produce an "optic" event that would provide motivation for them to follow through and change his perception of them. They left Simeon as they had left Joseph all those years ago. Yet, this time, they had opportunity to right the unspeakable wrong and reconcile themselves to their father and brother—even though they still did not know who he was. To them, he was just Pharaoh's enforcer. When God provides the setting and prospect for reconciliation, He depends on human players to play their parts in the drama otherwise known as life in real time. Humankind cannot gain substantive change if they neglect the divine chance for a realistic escape from the *trappings* of their old nature to the *transformation* of the new. God doesn't show up with a truckload full of new insights and just dump it on those in whom He seeks to bring transformation. He invites us to a level field where everyone has opportunity to participate and clear the air of all the resentment and bitterness produced by poor decisions. God's goal is not our comfort but our conformity. Things usually get sticky during a process involving righting wrongs and balancing old accounts. The product of God's process in redemption always brings necessary healing and needful understanding.

Then they all lived happily, ever after! Well . . . not quite yet.

> *"Then Joseph gave a command to fill their sacks with grain, to restore every man's money to his sack, and to give them provisions for the journey. Thus he did for them. So they loaded their donkeys with the grain and departed from there. But as one of them opened his sack to give his donkey feed at the encampment, he saw his money; and there it was, in the mouth of his sack. So he said to his brothers, 'My money has been restored, and there it is, in my sack!' Then their hearts failed them and they were afraid, saying to one another, 'what is this that God has done to us?"* (25-28)

Just When They Thought it Was Safe

While the granary stewards were loading their grain, Joseph secretly gave the command to place each man's money in the bag with the grain. He wanted to kill two birds with one stone. First, he wanted to provide for them in their obvious lack. He had the means to do so and he decided to use this occasion to refund money they spent to buy the grain. Additionally, he used this opportunity to keep them on a short leash—insuring their return and keeping the "fear of the Lord" in their hearts. When they stopped to make camp that night, each man found his moneybag in the sack of grain. They just stood there staring at their money wondering what else could go wrong in this bizarre adventure. So . . . what do they do? *They blame God.*

For years, their sin went unconfessed, unpunished, and unnoticed. I do not think they lived in glee as they had watched their father lament the loss of Joseph. I rather suspect that the guilt associated with the event continually ate at them. Now they stand speechless around the campfire wondering why this particular search for food has taken such unpredictable twists and turns. I can see them shaking their heads in amazement that their sin had been uncovered and judgment day loomed within striking distance. They all knew one thing. Their father would not take kindly to the possibility of losing his youngest son . . . again! While in Egypt, Joseph made sure they knew their place in the pecking order. Now that they were en route home, they began to focus on a more immediate problem—persuading their father to obey Joseph's command that Benjamin accompany them on their next trip for grain.

During the exact time they were dealing with the guilt as consequence of a wrong decision, Joseph faced a similar struggle to come to grips with the process of *forgiveness*. The chance meeting with his brothers came out of the blue like a meteor crashing into his neat and predictable world in which he only had to speak a command and mountains moved. He did not anticipate being knocked off his axis by the emotional storm he now experienced. While Joseph fully understood the significance of his present position in Egypt and God's role in placing him there, he also began to acknowledge that what God was crafting in his life did not end with his being elevated to second-highest in the land. God's intent was redemption and reconciliation. Joseph slowly began to realize that God's weaving of various colors and textures into his life's tapestry included being reunited with his family and providing a future and a hope for his race. Only God could do something so incredible! There is no waste in God's economy. Every incident attaches itself to other incidents like a linear chain of inter-related events designed to showcase God's sovereignty and providential plan.

Gaining a Clear Understanding of Guilt and Conviction

As I consider the situation, there are two sides to this topic of guilt and forgiveness. Guilt must be distinguished from conviction. Guilt comes from Satan and is intended to destroy. Conviction is the result of the Holy Spirit's work in us and is intended to give life. It is a part of God's plan of redemption.

If the guilt of something that happened in your past continues to eat at you, confess it to the Lord. Confession is the first step in ridding yourself of its effect upon you. If your guilt is the product of something out of your control, then recognize it as false guilt and tactic of your soul's enemy, Satan. But if the Holy Spirit is convicting you of an act for which you were responsible and which resulted in the untrue or unfair treatment of someone else, you need to ask God to forgive you of this trespass and make it right with the one you hurt. Everyone has moments when they rehash the past. The "what ifs" abound and torment the rational person with irrational thought and guilt associated with some particular event or encounter that went bad. "What if I had not reacted like that? What if I'd been where I was supposed to be?" On and on. The enemy of our soul wants to keep us bound to those tormenting questions, but the love of God cuts the rope and assures us of His forgiveness. Time to move on. Time to quit listening to the liar of liars and accept the unconditional love of the Lord of Lords.

Doing Life in Real-Time:

1. Forgiveness must be our goal.

   We are to forgive unconditionally, even though whoever hurt us may not admit they wronged us or ask our forgiveness. When you choose to forgive, you diffuse the bitterness bomb. *You cannot withhold your forgiveness until they acknowledge their wrong against you.* You can only control *your* actions and reactions. Don't allow yourself to be put in prison to them.

2. Forgiveness is an act of the will.

   It is not dependent upon how you **feel**. It is your decision to give it to God and get on with life. It is normal to experience negative emotions during the process, but they can actually serve as reminder of God's deliverance.

3. Pray for God's strength to forgive but leave the accounting to him.

Determine ahead of time that you will let it go. Forgive. But, pray that God would orchestrate a just resolution in the matter. Trust Him to bring it about in His time. Be careful not to let your prayer for justice become a revenge-seeking cancer in your soul.

4. Pray for those who have not acknowledged wronging you.

If you will pray for their spiritual condition, you will allow the Holy Spirit to reveal Jesus to them. Once revealed, He will have opportunity to change their life and you will have had a part in releasing them from the worst prison of all—the prison of sin. Only the Holy Spirit can speak to a man's heart about essential issues of life.

5. Write the names of those you need to forgive and who need also to forgive you.

Be intentional about the process and understand that God may be using you to help weave part of their life's tapestry. His desire for them mirrors His desire for you—a masterpiece made in His image. Yours is not the only tapestry in process right now.

Here's Your Handle:

Stop letting the people who wronged you live rent-free in your heart.

Chapter 8

"But God Meant It For Good"

The last chapter spoke of two things that often occupy different sides of the same coin. One is guilt; the other is forgiveness. We noted how, in the instance with Joseph and his brothers, they experienced the mature effects of long-term guilt and Joseph had to work through some emotional strawberries (or rug burns) at the same time. He had to take the second step in receiving emotional healing from what his brothers did to him.

A brief review:

1. As a young man, his older brothers despised Joseph because he was his daddy's favorite son.
2. Joseph had dreams of prominence over his brothers (and even shared these dreams with them).

3. His brothers have enough! They conspire and sell him to a caravan headed for Egypt, then lie to their grieving dad.

4. Potiphar—captain of Pharaoh's security guards, buys Joseph at the slave market. Potiphar's wife tries to seduce Joseph. Joseph resists on several occasions. Finally, after exhausting her seductive charm and realizing she could not prevail and that continued efforts could actually end up making her look desperate, Mrs. Potiphar cries "rape!" Joseph is framed and imprisoned—for *being* a person of integrity.

5. While in prison, Joseph interprets dreams for two of Pharaoh's closest staff that had fallen out of grace with him then imprisoned.

6. The butler was restored to his position, but conveniently "forgot" about Joseph. The baker lost his head.

7. Joseph interprets Pharaoh's two dreams. God speaks to Pharaoh. Joseph becomes Governor of Egypt and administrates the distribution of food and wealth in Egypt.

8. Because of the famine, Joseph's brothers come from Canaan to buy grain. He recognizes them and begins the process of finding out if his father and younger brother were still alive.

At this juncture in the narrative associated with the providence of God, I'd like to speak about what it takes to rebuild betrayed or broken trust. Most people have to work through betrayal at one time or another. Its process usually produces a new level of pain and the residual effect of opening a festering sore exposes frayed nerve endings to the air—like rug burn on steroids! Just when you thought it was safe to let down your guard, you get gut-punched again by the reminder of the original offense that produced seemingly endless mental pain, self-examination, and a futile attempt to diffuse the bitterness you feel. What you have experienced is really a de-callousing of self-protective flesh you developed over time to dull the pain and memory of the event. You built layers of callous over the injury and now the pain begins all over again. It arouses from its dormancy and plays like a vengeful sequel to your most prolific horror story. You discover that your healing process is far from complete and that the real work is yet ahead. You successfully numbed yourself from its crippling pain, but you discover that it never went away at all. It's been there—buried but very much alive.

Back to square one, except this time you have the accumulated repertoire of feelings and what they can do to you during the quiet times when it's just you and your mind—fighting battles in an imaginary battlefield. You think of all the things you could have said—or *should* have said. You question again the same things you once questioned but never gained an acceptable answer. Now that it's out in the open again, how will you respond to its revelation or its possible agenda?

It is said that the most vital ingredient in all human relationships is trust. Without it relationships fall apart, churches split, businesses fail and friends are alienated from one another. Once trust is broken, healing is essential. If the cohesive ingredient in the relationship is lost, only pieces of what was once beautiful and functional remain. Gaining forgiveness is divine. God produces the necessary capacity in the human heart to allow it to take place. Even so, the memory remains and the temptation to bail out of the process comes and goes. Yet, God brings the healing and forgiveness prevails. But, in the process of regaining trust, only human players can act out the script of repair and renovation. God leaves that part up to us—proving again that we can be trusted and that we learned the lesson of what betrayal can produce in an otherwise healthy relationship.

Joseph's relationship with his brothers provides

the classic narrative in God's Word dealing with restoring trust. We placed it under our microscope several chapters ago but still have not seen the entirety of what God wants us to see. Throughout the narrative outlined in this book, we recognized several issues that keep the human heart from alignment with the Father's heart. This chapter gives sufficient language in identifying things to look for in our effort to detect our offender's genuine remorse or if their effort to rebuild trust is still just an effort to conceal their own sordid agenda. Do they really want to rebuild trust or do they need another win in their column of self-justified actions? In a sentence, I want to show you how this chapter will be helpful—perhaps give hope—in places where your trust has been violated and your world shattered into a pile of shards.

In spite of the deep hurt, it is possible to restore trust and experience healing.

In order for Joseph to once again believe and trust his brothers, he needed to know two things:

1. That they were being *completely* honest with him;
2. That they were *truly* sorry for what they did to him and their father;

As Joseph's brothers returned home, they shared

every detail of what had happened—including the governor's demand to meet the youngest brother as proof that they were telling the truth and, indeed, were not spies. Jacob asserts his sentiment in the matter. *"You have deprived me of my children. Joseph is no more and Simeon is no more, and now you want to take Benjamin. Everything is against me!"* (42:36).

In his book, *Joseph: A Man of Integrity and Forgiveness*, Chuck Swindoll describes this sentiment as "the groanings of a sad dad." Jacob gave every indication that he still held his older sons responsible for the loss of his trophy son. It is hard to imagine the pain that Joseph's brothers also felt at the overt rejection and continued insinuation of guilt projected by their father. Like the deliberate act of planting *weed* seeds in a garden, such a continuing diatribe can only produce the growth of resentment and despair in the lives of those for whom it was intended. Whether or not Jacob *understood* the power of his words, they had a continuing erosive effect on his remaining sons. If he wanted them to feel unworthy of his love, they were certainly getting the message— played over and over again.

Myriads of families deal with this exact issue. Parents hold surviving siblings responsible for the loss of a brother or sister. While their words may not state their feelings exactly, their actions insinuate that they would rather have the child they lost instead of the one they have. They do great damage to the child's potential of becoming a productive member of society as they grow to adulthood under the cloud of covert rejection by their parents. The seeds of subtle rejection grow to maturity and shape the perspective they have—both of their parents and their own children. Instead of telling his sons he loved them and prayed for their safety each day, Jacob cut the bonds of affection and produced a family of scapegoats to justify his failed expectations. The same scenario exists in current society wherein a son or daughter tries desperately to gain the approval of his or her parents, but always ends up disappointed and subtly rejected again.

Parental approval provides healthy perspectives in children who are fortunate enough to take that cue from Mom or Dad. Parental *disapproval* provides enough seeds to spawn a garden of misguided actions and attitudes. Wisdom acknowledges that all seeds grow—whether or not they were the seeds a parent intended to be planted. Sometimes an insinuation can paint the wrong picture in the malleable mind of an adolescent or pre-teen and the wrong seeds grow to fruition. Their perspective grows into a reality in which they begin to play the role of how they *think* their parents perceive them. Maybe the seed that was planted and grew came from an old bag of seeds that one of the parents still had in the recesses of their own ledger of disappointments—a bag full of poisonous seeds *they* inherited.

I know a man whose father left his mother when he was a young boy. *Rejection number one.* His mother remarried several times and each time he trusted her less and less to provide the safety and affection every child deserves. Finally, the man who stayed with her the longest planted some poisonous seeds in his life. The stepfather told him that he would never amount to anything and that he was destined to be a loser. *Rejection number two.* Can you imagine hearing that message over and over again? While we may conjecture that the stepfather brought nothing into the marriage except his own agenda (which did not include children), the fact remained that he did irreparable harm to his stepson with his poisonous words. That stepson struggled for most of his life with that assessment of his character and potential. He tried desperately to prove his stepfather wrong as he wrestled with gaining a healthy self-image. Finally, in his adult years, he bought a franchise and began his own business. Things began looking up for him and his young family. On the outside, he mirrored a healthy individual. On the inside, he still wrestled with his stepfather's words and his mother's failure to protect him from his verbal programming.

As Reuben felt the impact of Jacob's despair, he told his dad that if he failed to bring Benjamin back, Jacob could put his two grandsons to death. Seriously? What grandfather would kill his grandsons? (Did I mention that this was a seriously dysfunctional family?) That is like saying, "If I cannot play this piano concerto perfectly—even though I cannot play piano, you can cut off my fingers." Not exactly an appropriate motivation. Who in their right mind would take a deal like that? A backwards glance at Chapter 35 might suggest that Jacob really did not trust Reuben since he had an affair with his concubine, Bilhah. Though that event took place several years earlier, apparently Reuben was still at work trying to rebuild his father's trust in him.

At any rate, it is Reuben who, as the oldest son, feels the responsibility for what he and his brothers did to Joseph—except he *still* cannot let Jacob know what *really* happened to Joseph and how he and his brothers continually felt the guilt of their actions. They determined long ago that the secret was one they must all take to their graves. Otherwise, they might have to deal with the guilt of seeing their father die from the impact of the deception they had to nurture to keep the family secret.

Initially, Jacob said "no" to their request to take Benjamin to Egypt. But, as food supplies dwindled, he had a change of heart. Judah, the fourth oldest son, pinch-hitting for Reuben, hit a run-scoring triple as he convinced Jacob to entrust Benjamin into his care. Jacob acquiesced to the lesser of two painful scenarios. Either keep Benjamin close and watch him starve to death or let him go with the slimmest of chances he would ever see him again. The brothers all returned to Egypt.

As they arrived back in Egypt, the stewards escorted them directly to Joseph's mansion (43:15-25). Given the nature of how things went on the first trip when they were accused of being spies, they assumed they would be charged with stealing the silver they found replaced in their grain sacks on the first trip home. They wasted no time in trying to set the record straight with the steward. They didn't know it, but this was a very wise thing to do. While their motivation derived from their penchant for self-preservation—perhaps even fearing an unforeseen reprisal from the Governor (Joseph), they set about to make sure the truth—or at least *their* version of it, was known before charges could be brought against them again. Unknowingly, they used the opportunity Joseph gave them to demonstrate honesty—the very aspect of their lives in question. The steward told them the account had been settled. They need not worry. Settled? What now . . . more imprisonment? Imagine their guilt-ridden minds thinking the worst—even though the steward had given them the "all clear." They suspected the worst because they were masters at deception and deceit. Was their own slight-of-hand now catching up with them?

When Joseph arrived at his home, his nervous and confused brothers were in place and had already laid out their gifts (43:26-31). They wanted to be ready for the Governor and possibly diffuse another of his outbursts by displaying their "peace offerings." I am reminded of the prelude to punishment suffered by my three sons. One of the three used the phrase, "I love you Daddy! I love you!" It was hard to punish a kid like that. Perhaps the brothers' display of their gifts was similar to my son wanting to diffuse my displeasure in his actions and diminish the severity of his pending punishment.

Joseph zeroed in on his greatest concern—his father. I suspect that he prepared his own heart to hear the worst and then deal with his brothers later. They reported that he was "alive and well." So far, so good. Joseph felt the cords around his heart loosen as he gave those words time to sink in. He was alive and well and the possibility of seeing him again began to emerge into the ray of hope he held in his heart since his "mysterious" disappearance. Imagine the questions that lurked behind his initial question. "Had his father missed him? Was it life as usual? What story had his brothers given their grieving dad and how could they live with themselves?"

Mirror, Mirror on the Wall

Then, Joseph looked directly at Benjamin. The last time he saw him, Benjamin was a one year-old toddler. He held no animosity toward him and probably even understood what it was like to be the youngest in the family with older brothers who all despised him for being the crown jewel of their father's virility. Joseph once held that designation and wondered silently if Benjamin had to endure the ridicule and rejection of his older brothers as he had. Perhaps not. Maybe they learned their lesson and, in some sordid way, decided that their previous attitudes would never again resurface and dictate their actions. Maybe they got caught up in their own emotions and feelings of second-rate offspring fostered by their father. After all, brothers talk. Their conversations about their family and its "crown jewel" probably took a left turn in the oft-repeated diatribes shared around the campfires at night.

Joseph said to them, "Is this your younger brother of whom you spoke to me?" Benjamin and Joseph had the same mother. Unlike the brothers who had disposed of him years before, they were not stepbrothers. They were blood brothers. At long last he had answers to many of the questions he held in this hopeful heart for years. His father was alive and his mother's other son was seated before him. As the realization set in, Joseph felt the dam breaking that held back all his emotions, confusions, rejections, and disappointments. His heart began to burst as the realization took its toll. He had remained composed as long as humanly possible. Then, when he recognized that he was about to blow his cover, he went to another part of his palace and wept. Torrents of tears flowed down his face as he allowed his emotions to rule for the first time in many years. Tears . . . cleansing tears! Hope restored in real-time. Joseph hoped for this day to eventually come, but he could not have known it would have this emotionally engulfing effect. He ruled over the greatest country on earth at the time. He made decisions every day that affected the lives of countless people. Everyone knew his authority and accepted his judgments and decrees. But now, he sat and wept like a baby as he tried to get a handle the greatest miracle of his life.

After an undisclosed amount of time, Joseph regained his composure and returned to his brothers and had them seated in order of their birth. When they were served, Benjamin received a portion five times greater than his older brothers. They took note and begin to wonder about the display of generosity by the Governor. Egyptian culture mandated generosity toward honored guests. Maybe this was one of those cultural things they did not understand but about which they were certainly curious. Joseph wanted to emphasize Benjamin's honor by giving him the larger portion. We can surmise that Joseph studied his brothers' body language and facial expressions as Benjamin was treated with such honor. Apparently, Joseph detected no jealousy . . . but there would be *one more* test.

Joseph noticed that *all* the brothers returned while only Benjamin was required to do so. *A good sign.* They *had* changed. Benjamin would not have to "go it alone" as Joseph had to over twenty years ago. Joseph could now be an advocate for him and make sure the same ill-conceived plans did not befall him.

While Joseph sensed a positive direction developing among his brothers, he decided to let things play out a bit further. After all, he held all the trump cards and could play them at will. He now controlled both his brothers' immediate situation and their future survival. Why rush the chest bumping and shoulder slapping? He wanted to reveal himself to his brothers but to do so now might short-circuit the whole process. If they had indeed changed, they would pass his last test. If not, his cautious instincts would prevail and other options emerge.

Same Song, Second Verse

Joseph commanded the steward to fill his brothers' sacks with grain and also to replace the money with which to pay for the grain. Then he told the steward to place his own silver cup into the sack designated for his brother Benjamin. At dawn, the brothers began their journey back to their home and to their father. However, Joseph instructed the steward to let them get a short distance from the city and then overtake them and begin a new line of interrogation.

As this vignette in the unfolding drama began to play out, the brothers maintained their innocence to the point of even saying the thief should die and that the rest of them would be the governor's servants. "What are you saying? Why would we take something from the governor after his generosity and kindness? You got us all wrong!" But when the cup was found in Benjamin's sack, they lost any confidence of winning this latest volley with the ruler of the land. As the steward brought them back to Joseph's house, they cringed as Joseph made his appearance. As he accused them of stealing from him and betraying his trust and good will, their self-assertion of innocence morphed into a full confession of the family secret. Judah owned up to their sin against Joseph. He also made it clear that they would not forsake Benjamin. If he had to be imprisoned, then *all* of them would be imprisoned. Judah acknowledged that it was God who uncovered their sin. *That was significant!* Since Joseph was presumed dead, it was their way of acknowledging God's intervention. To them, it was at long last time to pay the penalty for their years of deception to their father and enmity against their long-lost brother.

As a final step, Judah pleaded with Joseph to let Benjamin and the other brothers go free while he remained in his brother's place as a slave. Finally. *TRUE REPENTANCE* ! ! Joseph's heart melted like butter on a hot stove as he witnessed their brokenness. Gone was their machismo and bravado. Gone was the last image he had of them just before they lowered him into the pit. Gone was their scheming and evil intent. He witnessed their silent abandon to all they had held in reserve. He would extract no more confessions. He heard what he needed to hear. He sensed their hearts crying desperately to end the torment that had been their unintended consequence for years.

The Power of Blind Trust

Blind trust emerges when the one being tested does not know about the test. Blind trust paves the way for future relationship repair and provides the atmosphere in which the injured party can be free of the negative emotions of revenge and self-justice. Joseph provided his brothers with every opportunity to set the record straight and to come clean about the secret that tore the family apart and broke their father's heart. He forced the issue and forged a healing. His wisdom guided the timing and his influence kept the process on track. God used him to providentially guide the survival of an entire nation and an entire race of people.

Trust can only develop in healthy relationships. Trust is precious and must be viewed as the glue that holds people and families together. When trust cannot be found, families fall apart and society suffers from the ripple effect of broken promises and shattered dreams. Nothing else has the cohesive effect that trust provides. Men and women put their lives on the line for those they trust.

Chapter 45 begins with one of the greatest acmes in human history. Joseph had all the Egyptians leave the room. He no longer had to test his brothers' honesty. He instinctively knew they wanted to confess their great secret and experience the freedom of total honesty. He also knew they were willing to pay the price for such freedom. At that precise moment, everything came into focus. It was time. He began to weep loudly. His brothers could not discern his intent as he demonstrated this peculiar reaction to their most recent altercation.

First, he accused them of stealing and flexed his authoritative muscle to intimidate them. Now, he cries. I imagine that they began to wonder if they were in the presence of a lunatic and had become the object of a madman's ranting. But something was different. The enforcers had left the room and they were left alone with him. They could easily overpower him if necessary, but they stood transfixed by his sudden display of emotion. I can imagine their reaction. *"Ok . . . let's see how this thing plays out . . ."*

His tears were tears of relief and joy—not suffering and pain. His wailing indicated just how difficult it had been for him to hide his own feelings and put his brothers through such a tough testing period. After an adequate time, he cleared his throat, wiped his eyes, and moved nearer to them within the room. They stood silent and afraid of what this unusual behavior might produce. They still had no clue as to what he intended to do to them. Then, as he looked into their forlorn faces, he said, "I am Joseph; does my father yet live?" WHAT? They stood paralyzed from the impact of his statement. Joseph? How? Why?

I cannot imagine the poignancy of this moment. If this were a TV series, this would be a good place to break for previews to next week's exciting episode. *Does Joseph punish his brothers? Do they run for fear of their lives? Tune in next week for the exciting conclusion!* I am sure Joseph knew they needed time to absorb the shock of what he just told them. After all, they reckoned him dead and had kept the story line the same for over two decades. Now . . . what could they say? He stood right in front of them. With the enforcers gone from the room, what did he intend to do? Can you feel the tension mounting? Can you see the looks on their faces as they attempt to determine their fate and what his next words will be?

When God's Plan Trumps The Best Laid Plans Of Men

Knowing the impact of his revelation to them, he tried to assuage their fears and put things into proper perspective. *"God sent me before you to preserve a posterity for you in the earth, and to save your lives by a great deliverance" (45:7).* He recounted how a giant seven-year famine gripped the region and that five years remained in which no planting or harvest could take place. He pointed out to them that they meant evil by their actions toward him, but God had actually used their decision to preserve life for them. He made no mention of his unjust treatment or prison time. He chose to focus on two things. First, he wanted them to know that they had played a part in God's plan. While they lived the daily nightmare of remorse for their unprecedented solution to the family's irritation by disposing of him, God developed Joseph to become a great leader as He wove into his life the strands of adversity and challenge. Second, Joseph wanted them to know that he intended to take care of them—despite their earlier treatment of him. He had the power to do so and, as they were about to see, he did so in elaborate fashion. Talk about shock value! God's endgame was about to emerge for all to see.

I ask you to imagine again with me. Let's leave the brothers to do the customary chest bumping and backslapping as they get reacquainted. Let's leave them to fully absorb this providential point in which their lives all again intersected and once again became a family.

Doing Life in Real Time:

1. When someone violates your trust, determine to set a course for reconciliation—even though you are the victim. Make it possible for someone to regain your trust by:

> a. Giving opportunity for discussion by the involvement of an objective third person; It might be a marriage counselor or mediator.
> b. Giving the violator ample opportunity to understand the gravity of the offense and how it impacted you;
> c. Accepting their request for forgiveness and determine that the two of you *will* go forward;

2. When you have betrayed someone else's trust:

> a. Determine that you will engage in rebuilding

their trust.

b. Proceed at the pace with which *they* are comfortable.

c. Ask for their forgiveness and acknowledge your trespass. Be patient with them as they process their emotional response to your request.

Trust is not something a person can bring about by edict. It needs time to regrow its roots and establish a pattern of predictable behavior. It grows in the garden of honest transparency and produces the fruit of protection and reliability. Once mature, it guides the relationship to its fruitful purpose and guards from the intrusion of repeated betrayal. Once regained, trust becomes the strongest force linking two people together. But, it takes time.

Here's Your Handle:

In spite of the deep hurt, it *is* possible to restore trust and experience healing.

Chapter 9

The Trap of False Assumptions

To this point, our story focused largely upon the relationship between Joseph and his brothers. You might even call it a "non-relationship." The previous chapter revealed how Joseph finally revealed his identity to his forlorn brothers after a series of illuminating tests to ascertain the motives of their hearts and discern the truthfulness of their story to him.

I would like to use the final chapter of this book to focus on Jacob, the father. We can learn a great deal about the power of false assumptions by re-focusing our attention on the father of this interesting clan. For years he had managed certain assumptions based on evidence given. His whole life rotated around the belief that his favorite child met with a disastrous ending. That assumption literally rewrote the DNA of his family's dynamics. Love for his remaining sons became strained—at best. Because of the circumstantial evidence they presented to him on that fateful day, a light went out in his heart.

We manage the affairs of our lives with a series of assumptions. We assume correctly that the sun will come up each morning. We assume the car will start when we twist the key. We assume our job will be waiting for us as we arrive to begin another day of work. We assume that established relationships would always provide the atmosphere in which we can be ourselves without pretense or pressure. We assume that our spouse would always love us and never allow someone's wandering eye to begin the process of wanderlust or enticement. We tend to trust things we take for granted and put little or no thought into their maintenance. So . . . we live assuming things will be as they were represented to us initially and even build a system of thought to justify our lack of investment into our assumption's cultivation or nurture.

False assumptions derail choice opportunities. Perception of the relative truth in a matter usually steers an individual's agenda—especially if their mental operating system utilizes an inaccurate understanding of how things will eventually play out. A false assumption has the power to keep an individual locked in the dark chambers of his/her mind and never know the liberating truth.

A False Assumption Meets Integrity: *A Modern Vignette*

The pace of the rush hour traffic slowed to a crawl and then to a dead stop. Horns began playing their usual obnoxious symphony and nerves strained to stay contained. Jockeying for lanes quickly became a test of nerves and courtesy as the morning's complement of Type A's made their presence felt. One such Type A honked at a middle-aged man trying to merge right. Then, he made an obscene gesture reinforced with unnecessary profanity. The man could only watch as the younger man inserted himself into the spot. Fortunately, the driver right behind the young man slowed, letting him merge.

Ten minutes later, the older gentleman entered the parking garage, found his designated spot, and approached the elevator. As the doors opened, he was surprised to see the elevator nearly full. Suddenly, from behind him, the *same young man* pushed past him and took the remaining spot. As the doors closed, he thought, "*That is the young man who flipped me off this morning.*" He smiled silently to himself and hoped the irony would play out to his favor.

Once inside his office, his secretary handed him a folder and said, "A young man is here to interview for the opening." After pouring himself a fresh cup of hot coffee and taking his place behind his desk, the secretary ushered the young man into his office. You guessed it—the rude young man from the traffic jam and elevator. The interview began with an introduction and a handshake. He motioned for the young man to sit in the chair in front of his large wooden desk. He smiled to himself as he watched the young man shift nervously in his seat.

He asked the young man several questions—all of which were answered to his satisfaction. He had graduated in the top three of his class, had impeccable credentials, seemed to be bright—but still had not been able to land a job nearly a year after school.

Finally, the man looked at the young applicant and asked, "Why do you want a job here? With your credentials and grades, I would have thought you'd apply at a larger firm." The younger man sat silently for a brief moment and then said, "It's been much more difficult than I had suspected it would be.

Most of my friends—even those who graduated below me—now have jobs they enjoy. But, I . . ." His eyes fell to the floor and his demeanor conveyed the impression that he had endured many disappointing interviews—with nothing to show for his efforts. He continued, "But I seem to always make the short list and then . . ."

"And then you don't get hired, right?" He paused to let his words sink in and then pressed his point. "This morning in traffic, I was the person in the blue car you flipped off. Do you remember? Then again at the elevator in the garage, you pushed past me—even after I had already been waiting." His words fell hard and the young man knew this would be one time he would not even make the short list. "That's not the kind of person I want to represent my company."

After a long moment, the young man lifted his eyes and looked directly into the man's face. "You are right. . . I'm sorry. . . I thought I was going to be late. I let the traffic get to me . . . I sincerely apologize," he said as he reached down to retrieve his case. "I won't take any more of your time. Thank you for taking the time to see me." He stood to leave, but the man said, "The interview is not over until I say it's over. Please sit," he said, motioning to the chair.

As the young man took his seat, the older man said, "I have more to say." As the two sat for a moment, he began, "You were rude and arrogant. That might be prerequisites for some jobs, but I stress building relationships with clients by living and working with integrity—putting the needs of others before my own—and giving an honest effort to making my little corner of the world a better place. I am interested in someone working here who represents the interests of this company and conducts himself in a manner that engenders my trust. Above all else, he must possess the integrity that demonstrates his desire to grow into a productive and useful part of this team."

The words seemed almost canned, except that the young man's attention was riveted to each word. *Why is he taking this time with me? Didn't I already kill this deal in traffic?*

Sensing he had made his point, the man leaned forward and said, "Young man, do you believe you have it in you to do that?"

Stunned at the sudden shift in the older man's composure, he now sensed something he had not sensed before, but he couldn't put his finger on just what it was. "Do you?" the older man pressed.

A glimmer of hope appeared out of nowhere as the man awaited his answer. "Sir, I don't know if I possess those qualities right now, but I'd like the opportunity to work under someone who does—if that makes sense . . I feel I have a lot to learn, and . . . I also feel I have a lot to offer," he said as his voice trailed off.

"Young man, thank you for your honesty. See, you do have the makings of the kind of person I'm looking for. You could have given me the answer I wanted to hear, but instead, you were truthful, you *showed integrity*," he said as he rose from his seat and extended his hand.

Thinking the interview was over and that he had just sealed his own fate, the young man rose and took the extended hand. The two shook hands and then the younger turned to leave.

"Oh, I have one more question for you," he said as the young man neared the office's door. "Can you start on Monday?" – From *"Integrity's Irony," 'Perspectives: A Different Look at Every-Day Issues' by Jim Beaird.*

You might say the young man was a victim of his own false assumptions—even though he deserved to be dismissed without further consideration. The older man saw something deeper than the younger man's caustic demeanor. He was willing to mine for the gold beneath the surface of the mordant exterior presented by the frustrated young job seeker. But, if the assumptions of the younger man had played out, no opportunity would have materialized. Likewise, if the employer had allowed his first impression assumptions to bias the interview, he might not have discerned the circumstances driving the young man's caustic behavior.

> ²⁵ Then they went up out of Egypt, and came to the land of Canaan to Jacob their father.²⁶ And they told him, saying, "Joseph is still alive, and he is governor over all the land of Egypt." And Jacob's heart stood still, because he did not believe them. ²⁷ But when they told him all the words which Joseph had said to them, and when he saw the carts which Joseph had sent to carry him, the spirit of Jacob their father revived. ²⁸ Then Israel said, "It is enough. Joseph my son is still alive. I will go and see him before I die" (45:25-28).

For more than 22 years, Jacob had lived under a false assumption—that Joseph was dead. Now, his older sons gave him the news that Joseph was alive and well in Egypt. This news should have been cause for their dad to rejoice and celebrate. Jacob had long since given up hope of ever seeing Joseph alive again—after all, allegedly he'd been ripped to pieces by an animal. Now, he was being told that he was alive and thriving in another part of the world. The bearers of that good news were none other than the "bad-news-brothers" who had tried unsuccessfully to dispose of their spoiled sibling. But, there was a qualifying element that gave them not only the right, but also the privilege of bringing the news to their father. Their brother had forgiven them! Who better than to be the bearers of joy!? Who better to bring a long-needed healing to the clan?

To illustrate the completeness of God's plan, I'd like to highlight a few facts to those who may be living under false assumptions—perhaps without even knowing it.

Fact One: Grace Replaces Disgrace

The providence of God's plan for all humankind involves clearing memories and cleaning out depressive thoughts emanating from certain tragedies. He wants us to move beyond the place wherein we became stuck and open our eyes to the completeness of His overall providential plan. He wants to show us where we allowed false assumptions to not only guide our thinking but also to partially shape our destiny. It is a work of His grace. He wants us to partake in full measure and experience wholeness of heart, mind and body. He wants to replace the painful memories with a glimpse of the tapestry He's been weaving in our lives throughout our journey through the valleys of despair. He wants to clarify the misinformation and dispel the deceit that produced the alternate reality by which we gauged our perspective of His dealings with us. But ultimately, an essential work of the Holy Spirit produces the necessary changes in hard hearts and clouded minds. He seeks to bring to remembrance the things that Jesus taught. John 14:26 says, *"But the helper, the Holy Spirit, whom the Father will send in my name, He will teach you all things, and bring to your remembrance all things that I said to you."*

God's grace exposes our false assumptions. Many people live for years under a false assumption that hope no longer exists. The absence of a window into an optimistic future keeps them locked in a dark place with no prospect of ever getting better. But, God's grace intrinsically works against anything designed by the enemy of our soul to rob us of clear vision and open hearts. An on-going effort by our Father produces varying textures of experience into our tapestry while preserving the destiny in which our function will be to bring Him glory and preserve our lives. He does not want us to live under the power of false assumptions. He desires that we live in an atmosphere in which forgiveness and forgetfulness may coexist.

Maybe, you once believed in the inerrancy of the Bible, but somewhere along the line you let someone or something convince you otherwise. Now, it's not that you reject God, it's just that you won't let Him get too close or control too much of your life. You say, "It's OK God, I've got this! I trusted you before, but that was naïve of me to think that you would do everything. I guess I will have to pick up the ball you dropped." Your words may not be exactly like the preceding ones, but you hold God and His dealings with you at arm's length while you try to figure out how to get on with life. A man once told me, "God and I have an arrangement. I don't ask him for much and he doesn't ask me for much." That statement grew from an increasing adherence to false assumptions that did not accurately reflect the veracity of the incident in question. An individual may *think* that God abandoned them in the middle of a crisis while in truth, their hard heart and misguided perspective influenced both their focus on life and their trust in God.

For twenty-two years Jacob had been convinced that one thing was actually true: *Joseph, his beloved son, was dead.* That was Jacob's conclusion based solely upon the circumstantial evidence of a bloody robe and alleged eyewitness account of the other ten brothers—who at that time, Jacob had no reason to doubt or mistrust. However, as time passed he began to listen to the raspy voices in the recess of his mind telling him things his sons would never dare tell him and instilling a general and growing distrust of them. It might have been their cavalier attitudes that surfaced so shortly after their bad news to their father. It might have been something else, but Verse 26 says, *"He believed them not."* Why? Just think. What if the most sensitive thing in your whole life was touched upon, and you realized that you had lived under a false assumption—for who knows how long?

By this time, Jacob had a well-nurtured mindset created to deal with his greatest loss and biggest disappointment. His survival mentality dictated that he not allow himself to entertain the "what if" thoughts that occasionally surfaced at inconvenient times. He would push those thoughts from his mind until it was easy to do so. His false assumption became the callous that protected his heart.

I would venture a guess that Jacob spent times of reflection upon the years prior to Joseph's ill-fated mission to check on his brothers at Shechem. The memory must have become an unwelcome memory more than once. My own father has been dead now for nearly 40 years. I don't think of the times he punished me (although I remember them!) I think of the times we played ball together or snuck over to the Daisy Dell Drive-In for one of their famous deluxe burgers and hearing him say, "Now don't tell your mom." I remember the day at a high school track meet when he pretended to be an official so he could get right down on the field and watch me break a 28 year-old school record. He was there! I'll never forget how he used to just "show up" and end up right in the middle of things. I cherish the fond memories and don't re-hash his mistakes. I nurture no false assumptions about my dad because he demonstrated qualities that every son yearns to see and feel in their father.

After the day the bad news came, Jacob apparently allowed the false assumption of Joseph's death to flavor how he treated his other sons. He had cherished the memories of watching his favorite son grow into manhood. He held so tightly to those memories that relationship with his older sons ceased to be fatherly and rather became patriarchal. He had the final word in family issues, but did not seek close proximity with them.

Verse 26 says, *"Jacob's heart stood still ... "* There was nothing in the world that he'd rather believe! Let's try to get inside his head for just a moment. "Joseph. Alive!? But a beast ... killed him ... 22 years ago. I've believed that all these years ... I've accepted his loss. It's hard to digest this news!"

For the last 22 years he'd lived a life with no hope of ever again seeing his pride and joy. During that time he undoubtedly looked back on his own life and concluded that since he *stole* the birthright from Esau, God would see to it that he went to his grave in sorrow. After all, you can fool people but you cannot fool God. He knew this in his heart but did not know how it would play out in his life.

Maybe you have spent months or years punishing yourself and living under the false assumption that God was letting you get your just desserts for something you said or did long ago. Somewhere along the line you lost hope and allowed that loss to amend your perspective of life.

It's a pity that Jacob didn't *hang on to the memory* of what Joseph told his brothers long ago and used it as hope that God would someday use Joseph for good. Rather, Jacob allowed his immense grief and disappointment to blot out the sun of new daily possibilities and appreciation of the family remaining with him.

Are you living under a false assumption? Even though you wouldn't admit it if you were, the way to know for sure is to ask yourself this question: "Have I lost hope? Have I given up on feeling the power of God's presence in my life? Have I quit watching for God's provision?"

The news that Joseph was alive caused Jacob to *once again* have hope. When he heard all the words Joseph had spoken to his brothers and all the carts he sent to transport them, he said, *"It is enough. I will go and see him before I die."* His hope was *alive* again. Grace replaced disgrace. For the first time in over two decades the family had an opportunity to shed the weighty garments of shame and disgrace that had resulted from their covert sin and deceit.

Fact Two: God's Blessing Requires that We Move from the Carnality of Our Existence to the Place He Provided.

Jacob had to say 'good-bye' to an old lifestyle and venture into the new and different. We might take another candid look into his heart and see that something had changed. Gone were the feelings of self-flagellation associated with his own deceit long ago to gain the blessing of his father over his brother. Gone was the need to keep looking over his shoulder and expecting God to punish him over and over again. The future held hope and reconciliation. Now that things were out of *his* hands, the family could be whole again.

Chapter 45:9-11 relates how Joseph had given the directive to his brothers to "get Dad and the rest of the clan and come back here to live. There are 5 years of this famine left." Jacob had to say good-bye to familiar surroundings. It was hard for two reasons. First, he was over 100 years old. His advanced age made it difficult to adjust to a new geographical and cultural change. Secondly, moving seemed to contradict God's word to his father and grandfather. It was *Canaan* that was to be the land of promise. Yet, he didn't argue. *"So Israel (Jacob) took his journey with all that he had . . "* (46:1).

The pragmatic side of us says, "So, how does this apply to me today? How is this relevant?" The relevance of Jacob's move is for both the Christian and the "not-yet" Christian. Phrases like, "believing in the power of the Blood of Christ," can strike the "not-yet" Christian with a sense of unease. Blood? But, if they ever choose to trust Christ to forgive their sins, it will be because they trust the power of the blood He shed at the cross. At first, it will be totally new to them. But as they begin to experience the peace they cannot explain and the acceptance they never before experienced, God will increase their appetite for all these new feelings and more.

I tell Christians that it will be a challenge to accept the *new* and *different.* It might be harder to get out of the rut of non-productivity for Christ than to chart a new course with a new sense of purpose and freedom.

Jonathan Edwards, who preached the classic sermon, *"Sinners in the Hands of an Angry God,"* said, "It is the task of every generation to discover in which direction the Sovereign Redeemer is moving, and then to move in that direction."

Up to this time, Jacob had been pre-occupied with the dismal nature of his own suffering, sorrow and self -pity. He lived an assumption based upon inconclusive evidence. But God's blessing required him to move from the sphere of the false and counterfeit to the sphere of truth and authentic provision. God's blessing awaited him there. Modern vernacular uses the phrase "getting out of one's comfort zone." Jacob had to leave his well-fortified safe house and move to the locale of God's blessing. That's where he would find Him.

God has a way of making the new and different an attractive alternative to the bleak and dismal past. The invitation is to each of us. Only we can make the decision to let go of our hurts and disappointments and to move ahead to where we can once again experience life as God planned. The tapestry God continues to weave for each of us can only be seen through obedient eyes. Once we catch a glimpse of the masterpiece of His making, we begin to understand that nothing has been wasted. There are no scraps on the floor. He uses everything in our lives to produce something useful to His kingdom.

My good friend Jim Beyer once used a phrase that sums up the whole issue of God's providence. In reference to Genesis 50:20 where Joseph told his family that what they meant for evil, God meant for good, he said, "God gives us 50:20 vision." We think we've been defeated, but God strategically placed us in the position to save lives. He intends to redeem our many mistakes and replace our morbid mentality.

If Jacob had not decided to move with God's plan, he could have remained in his pity party and said, "I will go to my grave believing a false assumption. It takes too much effort even to accept the truth after all these years." But God made Jacob a promise a long time ago when He said, *"I am with you and will keep you in all places wherever you go, and will bring you up again into this land"*(Gen. 28:15).

During all these years he may have wondered what it meant when God said, "I will bring you again to this land." If he was to be brought again to this land, it meant he'd first have to leave it. Jacob's mind began putting things in sequence. Maybe God hadn't forgotten him after all! Could Joseph really be alive? Wow! The new and different began to appeal to him like never before. It was as if God was saying, "Go ahead. Go down to Egypt. What I said I'd do, I'll bring to pass, except you have to be in the *right place* to see it."

If you are in God's family, you have this guarantee: Your worst failure can be turned into your greatest success. Why? Because you are God's child. You are a joint heir with Jesus Christ. God will honor His Son. Do you know what that means? Anything that *happens* to you or *touches* you becomes God's problem. We can say it another way. Anything that happens to you must first gain God's permission. Either way, God's grace always trumps disgrace.

Doing Life in Real Time:

Can you identify some assumptions by which you evaluate relationships that have not proven to be authentic? If so, how have you attempted to make things right?

    a. Set a time and place for a face-to-face meeting and give permission for open discussion.

    b. Determine ahead of time that you will listen fully to their version of what they perceived to have happened. You might be surprised.

    c. Seek understanding and extend or receive forgiveness.

Here's Your Handle:

Only you can make the decision to let go of your hurts and disappointments and to move ahead to where you can once again experience life as God planned. God provided the exit door to your self-imposed prison, but it's up to you to use it.

--- EPILOGUE ---

Providence Factor: Lessons From A Delayed Flight

I was in the middle of a busy week of travel. I sat in an airplane in Colorado Springs waiting for a lightening storm and torrential downpour to run its course so our plane could take off. My stomach tightened as the storm's duration ate into my layover time in Denver. The storm eventually passed and our plane taxied to its designated runway. I glanced at my watch and absorbed the probability of having to catch another flight out of Denver—probably not until the next morning. That meant more hotels and shuttles back and forth—unpacking and then packing again in a few short hours. As our plane arrived in Denver, those of us with connecting flights were allowed to deplane first. I ran to my gate only to find the door closed and the breezeway being positioned away from the plane. That meant my anxiety was prophetic.

I debated whether or not to catch a shuttle to a hotel or call my son in Denver. I decided to call my son and he graciously arrived soon after to pick me up and take me to their home for the night. During the next several hours, we talked and bantered about everything from politics to Facebook pet peeves. Then, as we both got ready to say good night and get some rest, he began to share perspective God had given both him and his wife during the last year in which their son had been diagnosed with a very rare and deadly cancer. Their previous year had been a year that most people might have given up and started blaming God for their misfortune. However, he shared something with me that I want to include in this writing. It is a story that needs to be told—a real life, hands-on perspective about God's providence that hits home in a way nothing else can.

Here's **his** story:

"We were completely exhausted. The humid Georgia summer heat had beaten us all day and we knew that the dinner meal only meant a short reprieve in the rigorous schedule. After seven days in the field, there was not a pleasant smelling guy in the bunch. Our heels were together habitually as we sat and shoveled the combination of peas, potatoes, gravy, and some kind of meat. No time for socialization in the five minutes between grabbing the plate from the server and dropping it off with the unfortunate soldier who got stuck with KP duty that day.

Back out the door and into the heat. Back to the equipment that had a week's worth of mud, filth, and carbon to clean off. The first hot meal in a week was already a distant memory and the watchful eyes of the drill instructors stung the backs of our heads almost as bad as the sunburns on our bare shaven scalps. Mortars, rifles, shovels, and everything that goes into war training needed to get spotless before a shower and bed was even a consideration.

The tire of the platoon was evident. The morale of the group was low. I imagine we looked like a slow motion film even though we were operating at our fullest capability. This was one of the moments in which I wondered what beach my friends were enjoying back home. This was one of the times that I really wanted, more than anything else, to just jump in a pool to cool off and then go fall asleep in front of a TV.

As our destitute faces became evident to the drill instructor, he quickly developed an eerily tranquil scowl. What he said next is the foundation for any perspective I have had since that point. "No matter how bad you think you have it," he barked in a voice that was obviously worn from several miles of marching cadences, "it can always be worse." Then, just to drive the point home, he made it worse for several more hours of push-ups, sit-ups, and flutter kicks before we could return to our tasks.

Army Infantry Training was where I discovered how deep I could truly dig when times get tough. It was painful and miserable, but my body and mind was conditioned to it. It was more about forming perspectives in circumstances beyond our control and finding the discipline to persevere through adversity. It was one of the pillars of **providential intervention** in my life that I now see with clarity.

Twenty years later, I found myself being escorted to a small consulting room at Children's Hospital Colorado with my wife, the surgeon, and his assistant. Our three year old son had just undergone a biopsy surgery for a lump that we had recently discovered in his thigh. As soon as we all sat down, I felt the somberness and realized that this was not a meeting where we find out that everything is going to be fine.

If ever there was a time when you would hope for fortitude to kick in, this ranks on the very top. No words were even needed and I don't think I processed more than three of them during the entire conversation. If you are a parent, imagine the horror of finding out that your child has developed an extremely aggressive and advanced malignancy so rare that there is almost no research data available.

For weeks after, both my wife and I notably seemed aloof and uninterested in conversations. We were disconnected from the world. The term, shell-shocked, might be the most accurate description—as in a war movie where a bomb explodes near a soldier and everything goes silent and he forgets where he is. Other soldiers are yelling at him, yet he does not comprehend any of it. He stares forward and looks at nothing with blank expression. He doesn't know where he is, he doesn't grasp what just happened. That was us—shell shocked.

Even once we moved past the shell shock phase, we moved to the place where we just wanted to not think about it every minute of the day. We didn't tell most people about it because we didn't want to have to talk about it and explain Sclerosing Rhabdomyo-sarcoma again. There would be times when the feelings subsided and we could focus on the normal world again – we found comfort in distractions. Things would be tolerable until someone asked something as simple as "how are you?" We would take a deep breath, muster a cordial response, and keep a poker face. Inside, the reminder that our life is anything but well released the pain again.

In this time of absorbing the surreal situation, Ali and I had reached the consensus that whatever the outcome, we will not place blame. We won't blame ourselves, we won't blame situations, we won't blame each other, and we won't blame God. We just took blame off the table entirely.

Surgeries, scans, chemotherapy, and radiation consumed our life for nearly a year. The petty problems that people complained about became offensive because we would give anything to trade for those simple problems. Unsolicited advice was arriving constantly from well-meaning people who didn't truly grasp the severity of his rare diagnosis and completely unknown prognosis. As parents, we were torn apart inside seeing our normally vibrant son succumb to a chemical that is literally intended to kill a part of his body in order to hopefully cure it. There are few people who really get to witness what chemo does to a three year-old's body. If you have never experienced it, count yourself lucky.

After a marathon year of fighting this battle, we got the answer that we had been hoping for at this time in the treatment cycle. Remission is the term, but cancer-free is what we celebrated. We threw him a pretty awesome party. There was a bouncy house, a chocolate fountain, and the local firefighters even showed up to help celebrate with a hundred or so friends, family, and neighbors.

Through the experience, the clarity of providence appeared brighter and more apparent than anything I have ever experienced. We quickly realized that the situations and experiences leading to this point were in no way coincidental. For me to list how everything lined up would be impossible. I would have to explain how everything was woven into place, complete with back stories and tedious details. The most effective way to explain it is this: If there was a divine entity that decided to make an awesome story, THIS IS IT.

1. In 2007, events in our life brought my wife and me to Denver, Colorado. Our son was born in 2010, followed closely by a beautiful daughter. We grew in our professional fields and have made great connections since. Those connections led us to points 3, 5, and 6 below. Being in Denver allowed for #2.

2. The Children's Hospital in Denver is ranked one of the best in the nation for pediatric oncology. The professionalism and knowledge of the staff to diagnose and treat such a rare

type of malignancy was monumental in the care of my son. There are fewer than 50 known cases of this variant and less than 10 pediatric extremity cases known to exist in the world. An attempt to rival this level of expertise while still living in Iowa would have required our family to be separated.

3. We struggled with the decision to proceed with radiation treatments due to the devastating long-term effects to the location and his age. It was literally a decision that could leave him with lifelong major surgeries and severely hindered mobility. I recalled having a neighbor with whom I played softball several years back who was in the radiation oncology field. I trusted her opinion and discussed the treatment and the reality of the situation. It turns out that she did her residency under the same radiation oncologist that we were working with in Denver. Her confidence in him was absolute. This assurance led us to proceed and we met unexpected and very unlikely good news during his treatment planning. As of the latest scans, our son has averted the scenario that could have left him with a lifetime of surgeries and pain.

4. I must keep it vague, but leading up to this chapter of our lives, we had many situations where we felt that we were robbed of certain opportunities. Looking back on those opportunities, it is evident that doors were closed to keep us ready and capable for this situation.

5. Ali and I had both just recently started new jobs. There was no realistic option for either of us to quit or take leave, so we needed to find a nanny to help with the logistics and care. Out of three million people in the Denver area, the first person we interviewed had lost a close cousin to a similar form of the same cancer. She understood the stakes and was able to assist with a heart of pure gold. She was able to create a level of comfort in our home that brought us peace when we needed it most.

6. Our new jobs gave us the flexibility to focus on the situation. Again, there are many details I am leaving out because they are so interwoven and too complex to explain. I was able to handle conference calls while holding my son in the infusion room. Ali was given

amazing leadership who understood our reality and let her step away when needed.

7. Prior to the symptoms appearing and before the diagnosis, I did the math and decided that, as a healthy family, we should opt for the much higher deductible health insurance plan so that we could get some financial relief with lower premiums. My gaffe in missing the deadline for submitting the forms saved about $10K in out of pocket expenses during the year of treatments.

8. The housing market was so crazy that we spent two years looking for something that would work for our growing family. We gave up on the perfect house and just wanted to settle for something without drunk bums on our sidewalk at midnight, literally. Houses would go on the market and have multiple offers the first day. At the right time, through unlikely people and circumstances, the right opportunity opened up and we were able to build the perfect house for our needs. We were moved in and settled just months before his diagnosis.

9. My dad was finishing his Doctoral program and I was working on my Master's degree. I wasn't in any mad rush to finish, however, he

mentioned that it would be great if we could both graduate in the same year. In order to appease his excitement, I doubled up on some classes and we enjoyed celebrating our respective graduations with each other. My last class ended a month prior to the diagnosis. Had I not accelerated my courses to finish earlier, I would have had the stress and financial obligations of an unfinished degree added to our situation. The added work load and deadlines also created an environment that summoned a mindset of discipline and urgency that would be necessary for the impending battles.

These instances, in addition to numerous others, came together in a supernatural mesh to bring a holistic healing to not only my son's physical needs, but to our family and our faith. **We are able to look back with amazement at a plan of providence for healing that was set in motion years before he was even born.** It is statistically impossible to attribute the sum of these situations and events to coincidence.

Difficult times do not fall into our paths as a punishment or for some sadistic cosmic reason. They are *expertly placed* there to help us realize who we are and what are our capabilities. The lesson from my drill instructor was that misery is not optional – our perspective of it, however, shapes us and builds our confidence for the times when mission success is critical. If we fail to look back and see that those hardships conditioned us for inevitable worse times, we miss the opportunity to be thankful of the fact that they were providentially placed to make us better people and serve a greater good."   - Jeff Beaird

Just as with Joseph, God arranged the events and locations in my son's life to coincide with their need to be in close proximity to the best cancer treatment available. EVERY step and stop positioned them to be at just the right place at just the right time. Only God's providence can orchestrate a human drama so intricate as that. What the enemy of our soul meant for death and evil, God turned around before my grandson was born. He began the chain of events eventually leading my son and his young family to be in the perfect scenario so that their son's life could be spared.

Had I not missed my flight, my son and I would not have had the conversation in which he expressed his gratefulness in a providential God for saving his son. THAT'S life in real time!

The tapestry of our life is woven with a variety of textures and colors. While we see only the knots and junctures on its back side, He uses everything to produce a masterpiece that will reflect what's in His heart. Nothing happens without His permission.

Remember,

God has a plan. He knows what's ahead.
He's shaping a world-changer.

Jim Beaird

ABOUT THE AUTHOR

Dr. Jim Beaird pastored for thirty years prior to becoming the Executive Director for the Southeast Region of Open Bible Churches in 2002. His passion is church planting and leadership development. He also authored *The Proximity Factor: Essential Disciplines in a Leader's Spiritual Formation* and teaches seminars to leaders and churches ready to maximize personal and corporate spiritual growth. He currently heads the Master's of Arts in Christian Ministry program at New Hope Christian College in Eugene, Oregon.

He and his wife, Kris, have three married sons. They reside in the Tampa Bay area and together enjoy the beach, target shooting, and walking.

His devotional writings can be found at www.jimbeaird.com.

Made in the USA
Coppell, TX
08 May 2022

77560429R00125